Chinese Wrestling

Kitchen Knives/Axes over China

Bill Xun Cheng
程迅

Chinese Wrestling
Copyright © 2019 by Bill Xun Cheng

Tellwell Talent
www.tellwell.ca

ISBN
978-0-2288-1895-3 (Paperback)

1

Chinese Wrestling

There are many kinds of wrestling: Turkish, Japanese, Mongolian, Korean, etc. Each one has its own name, but my poor language skills allow me to call them all by one name: wrestling.

There is also Chinese wrestling, which is the most common type, and is popular among children and adolescents. Whether they are playing or fighting, the wrestlers pre-emptively grab each other's clothes at the shoulders, and they pull them into their arms. The tricky children know how to use their feet to make their opponent unstable, losing their body's center of gravity, that is, to make them fall. Both sides are pulled down, followed by a series of crushing and rolling maneuvers. Neither combatant will concede defeat. Staying on top is not easy, either. At any moment there is the possibility of being overturned. Exerting pressure makes one feels like he might be the winner.

Lower your arms, hug your opponent's waist, often while being hugged by him, so both sides began to twist. Waist strength is the key to victory. Drop your arms and grab your opponent's leg, causing him to jump on the other one. He can be dropped at any time, and his own weight will pull you down to a fall. Before you both fall to the ground together, some terrible tricks may occur, like the locking of the neck. Clamp your opponent's head under your armpit, keep your left and right hands tightly locked together, and sit down on the ground. Your opponent must be head-down, buttocks up, and the limbs can no longer be forced. This ground wrestling can put you both in the same position—your bodies twist and cannot be judged as winner nor loser, but due to the momentum, locking the neck does not have any advantage.

Here is another strategy: a little advanced action over the shoulder. Do not let your opponent wrap around his own body, but pounce on him at his lower waist, take a hold of the other side of the body so that it can be lifted, and then place your hands on his back and push. Your opponent will fly over your shoulder and onto his back. This is called a "small move." With this strategy, your opponent can't wrestle, and it works every time. Confront your opponent and try to lower his upper body, then suddenly get up and lift their whole body. Your opponent must face down from your back and slide to the ground, his two feet in the air. You are the winner. Let your opponent's "dog eat"; in other words, put his face to the ground.

This "big back throw" is not real combat. I have never seen it. In my childhood, we were called to go to the countryside nearby to perform work in the fields, to learn and get ready to become agricultural labourers later. We had a very proud name at that time: "the poor and lower-middle-class peasants" or the "commune members." As general labourers, we were in the field to pick up wheat spikes, to collect the dropped wheat and bring it to a courtyard, where it was further processed. Our activity centre was the courtyard, this is an event location. Straw, hay was not rolled and packed. Roof-high straw was placed together to form a huge cushion. It was ideal for us kids to practice wrestling. We also learned the basic skills of wrestling. There were children being taught in a secret place, and they were likely to show us a few tricks. Unlike me—I am not a skillful wrestler. I fell every fight.

To enter the threshold of competitive wrestling, you must learn to fall first. If any part of your body touches down the ground in a fall, it will not hurt you. Go ahead with the wrestling you love; I've been beaten enough. I quit.

After all, wrestling is fair play. In the game you don't punch. You don't use weapons. You take one opponent at a time to fight with. All the other activities I mention below are not fair.

Read a nursery rhyme, entertainment first:

> Let's go.
>
> Fall a big horse on the ground.
>
> The horse didn't fall well.
>
> It broke his waist.
>
> Please go to see a doctor.
>
> You've got a needle.
>
> And take the medicine.
>
> Why didn't you cure in three days?
>
> Laugh! Laugh!! Laugh!!!

After reading the nursery rhymes, we would all hold back and try not to laugh. Whoever laughed first would lose the game. The loser would be punished. The winning child held the loser's hand while playing the above-mentioned nursery rhyme and spanked the hand with rhythm, again and again.

Ever heard of team wrestling? Not a group fight, but "riding a horse to war." One child is a horse, carrying another child to battle another such pair of people: horse and knight. This is a battle of high body-muscle energy consumption. Very often "two-legged horses" met single ones, and barehanded knights fell to ground quickly, a one-round game.

Ever heard of a donkey ride? Two teams of children choose the captain by playing stone, scissors, cloth, and the loser starts as the donkey's head. His team becomes the donkey. One by one, the team members bend over, heads against their teammate's buttocks in front, to form a long donkey back. The winner's captain is the "pioneer"; he takes a few steps to speed up, then jumps into the air, splits his legs, and jumps onto the donkey's back near to the head. All members of the winning team take turns jumping, flying, landing, and riding the donkey. Without the donkey collapsing, the captain on the donkey's back challenges the donkey's head with rock, paper, scissors until the next round when the other team gets a chance to ride the donkey. After losing several rounds in a row, the donkey's head must be beaten or fired by his own team members, and then they change the donkey's head to a kid they fell will bring them good luck, and they continue to play. This donkey-riding game is much more exciting than the jumping horse in competitive gymnastics. In jumping horse, the athletes are using equipment; while riding donkeys, our thin bodies fly up and hit the donkey's back. We use real human bodies in an almost abusive game that we play for fun, so this game is called "Hammer the Donkey."

Sandbag shooting is a game of running, stopping, and turning around. It is a test of body coordination. Children, both male and female, can compete in mixed teams. The playground is flat and separated by 8–10 metres of two lines. The attacking team splits into two lines, the shooting/throwing sandbag team against the defending team, and the defending team runs back and forth between the two lines, trying not to be hit by a sandbag. One player is a "duck" when hit by a flying bag. One can catch the flying bag and save a life, or get an additional chance for themselves, which means the side-out of a teammate can return to the field to continue running and dodging or bagging to participate in the game before the side exchange. Failure to catch the flying bag or dropping it on the ground counts as a hit. The whole defending team is hit or killed one after another until they run out of players, then the sides exchange.

This game is like baseball, but it's much more intense. On the attacking side everyone is a pitcher. Picking up bags and delivering them to the side's more lethal pitchers also reflects team spirit. And picking up the sandbag when the flight of the bag was caught by the other side also does not count. So, in the bag pick-up action, the player has to shout out "bag delivery!" to avoid disputes. The pitcher specifically aims at the other side of the children's legs, because the defending kid cannot catch the bag using his legs to gain points. Imagine ten children in the middle nervously ducking, running back and forth, even colliding, falling; two lines outside the attacking side's children, five on each side picking up the bag, the delivery of the bag, dropping the bag, shooting the bag, etc.

Children who are out of the game are often those who are slightly less physically coordinated and get hit by a bag easily, or they drain all their energy and fall to the ground, allowing them to be hit at a closer range. While serving as a bag picker, the bag carrier is not strong nor old enough to the shoot a fatal bag, which gives the opposite side extra chances.

2

Barbed Wire Can Be a Toy-Making Material

What did we have then? We had nothing. It's an irresponsible answer. We still had something to play with. We had barbed wire. There were ponds in the summer that could be wild swimming pools, while in the winter they could be wild ice rinks. We had small knives. I probably using more tools than any of the other children, such as tiger pliers, screwdrivers, hammers, saws, or whatever, and an antique that no one plays with nowadays: a calculator ruler. Sliding the calculation ruler, performing BEDMAS (Brackets, Exponents, Division, Multiplication, Addition, Subtraction) is something I could do, since I was a child of university staff parents.

In a popular ballet musical at that time, *The White-Haired Girl*, Yang Bai Lao, the dad worked in vain all his life. Why? Because he couldn't perform this calculation. He had to put his daughter, the loner heroine Shi-Er, into Mr. Huang's family as a maid to pay off his debt. In fact, I am so useless, in the end, that my daughter got married. She also married into the Huang family!

I had a pair of tiger pliers, also known as flat-mouth pliers. It could cut a #8 wire, but I was an eight-year-old child. My hand did not have the powerful gripping force needed to cut #8 steel wire. I could often only scratch a mark on the wire and then bend it back and forth until the wire split apart. Its cross-section is irregular; no micro-grain, crystal, or crystal layer fracture of the scientific image/metallography would appear. I cut off this piece of barbed wire, took it home, and stripped off its iron thorn and iron quinoa one by one. The other pliers of mine had a peaked head, and the iron thorn from #10 wire is slightly soft, but they were too short, and its sharp end was not good, and the wire would slip away from the pliers. Then would come a few drops of blood and pain from my wounded hand.

I wanted to join the air force, because I heard you were not only able to fly an airplane, but there was also a chance to ride on a spacecraft. These hand wounds diminished my courage to sign up, because it is said that, as a pilot, one cannot have any scars on his body, not even a tattoo.

Then again, some people preferred to use a hammer to straighten the curved barbed wire, but I rather liked to use pliers instead. Pliers can bend the wire, or they can straighten it. Pliers slowly straighten the wire, with or without stress built in. To phase the structure or grain, the composition of the wire changes as little as possible. There are some changes in the organization of the phase: there will be either softening or hardening of the whole wire, or part of it. To obtain this knowledge you must practice; you go and bend pieces of wire. And you will master it, too. Do you still not understand? You may not have an easy time working in the metal fabricating industry.

The material is ready, so making a homemade toy is next. What kind of toy to make? Cold weapons, slingshots, hot weapons, match guns, handguns … boys must have things, and I made them all at home. Slingshots were the simplest. The materials for making it were easy to find: a stick, a stethoscope hose, and rubber strips are good materials; also, a piece of real cowhide to fabricate the rock/ball pocket. With a good slingshot I had made, I went to find a shooting master among the children, one who could shoot down birds in the wood, hit a sparrow or something. Zhang Qing is an idol in our hearts. He could beat the greatest idol of all, the sexy monk Lu Zhi-Shen. Sometimes with your idol, the best way to copy him is to make and use his weapon.

3
Badges

At the beginning of the Cultural Revolution in China in 1966, the school-run factories began to go crazy, and the Chairman encouraged badge production. On delicate aluminum sheets, they painted Chairman Mao's head like a medal. What is the point of having one piece per head in China? Circulation, according to conservative estimates, is also comparable to the issue of RMB coins. You look back at the early days of the Cultural Revolution, and you see there are many poor penniless ghosts, but the chests that were not wearing Chairman Mao's medal were not easy to find. Because China is a large country with a large population, the Cultural Revolution began with 700 million people and hundreds of millions of badges given out, in just less than a year's time, for almost free to the whole country and even the world. Badge production workshops and artisans became sought-after goods—fashion, popular staff were not comparable to it. The standard or ideal badge position is on the left side of the chest, a Chairman Mao medal with his smiling face on it, and he is wearing a military-green hat with a red star. Below it would be a rectangular "Service the People" badge. This combo was just fine. More than two was showing off. The star-shaped medal was difficult to find, because the vice-commander of the military, Lin Biao wore this, and in China the red star is the symbol of the military. It can also be substituted with an oval medal, but the rectangular "Serve the People" badge must be original, because Premier Zhou Enlai wore one, with a white background and red lettering: "Serve the People." How to paint red on a medal? With a medical syringe injector, to extract the red paint. Inject red paint into the medal groove on the module, then take it to the oven and dry it with infrared light, which is as effective as Jingtai blue.

As to why was there no Jingtai blue process applied to Chairman Mao's medal? Who would use the pure artificial process of Jingtai Blue, a very Chinese artwork, at that time? I am indulging in infinite loyalty to Chairman

Mao, but a common feature of the production of the finished Chairman Mao medal, issued to the hands of the individual, is that there was absolutely no reprocessing of post-production transformation. The degree of loyalty to him then is indescribable, a kind of challenge at that unusual time, perhaps slightly modified or touched-up; that is, there was a suspicion of being one of the counter-revolutionary criminals. More than one thing is not better than one thing less, according to Chinese philosophy.

People quickly changed their hands-on and creative abilities, switching to making sofas and wooden furniture. Before and after a marriage license was issued, you could get a permit to buy a large wardrobe, but that did not mean that you could buy one, and buying one did not mean that it could be transported home. If it was a three-layer board, or a better five-layer board in material, with a double or triple door, including a glass door or a better mirror-door wardrobe, usually the happy buyer would have to borrow a three-wheeled staple cart to bring it home. I, to be able to get married later, learned how to ride three wheels—what one might call a tricycle—first. A cotton rope, a cotton quilt or blanket, was put on the top of the bundle on the three-wheeled cart. Behind it was the wife following on a bicycle. You would be happy to see that she drove her own bicycle with one hand while the other pushed the tricycle to get the wardrobe all the way home, intent on looking as if I was escorting her to carry the spoils for her.

The captives. Shanghai went back to the city's young intellectuals, the young generation, simply gave up the queue and returned to the city. Among them there was a boy who actually made his hardwood floor with his family's and neighbor's limited monthly amount of firewood tickets. He bought wood to chop, and one by one assembled it all into a wooden floor tile in a new room. He laid the solid wood floor while maintaining his family's and neighbor's stove to save him using wood. What is this brain? What is this heart and what is this craft? How many young girls would chase him? A love for a handyman. He was my idol.

What's electrical power tooling? We had none. The lamp? Homemade. The fluorescent light? Self-assembled. The radio? Homemade. The television set? Homemade. Can't afford it? Make a TV accompaniment; you can at least listen to the TV programs instead of watching them. FM radio? No need, because at that time even FM radio stations did not exist. FM radio sending and receiving began in mid-1980. I only demolished my single bed in 1980 (because I was a student and I—just like all other university students—had a bed in a college dormitory for free). My bed at my parents' home had no use then, with its wooden planks and homemade dividers. I bought a high-frequency head and a state-of-the-art rubber-side wrap paper bass with large-calibre sub-woofers and I made a speaker box. I only built one box, because the money or budget was tight and I could not afford to build two speaker boxes. Secondly, radio, tape, or records were mono. There was nothing called stereo. A year or two later, my father brought home a home hi-fi stereo set from West Germany, as well as some stereo records, including Beethoven's First to Ninth Symphonies conducted by Karajan. From then on it became my asset in chasing girls. I made a cover with white silk on its upper part surrounded by a special fabric decorated with gold-red fine wire called Malik—it looked just like a statue of an Arab prince. But the halal religions in the Arabic world do not allow them to shape figures or images of God. According to my mother, my dad got this high-end home entertaining center, the Hi-Fi tower, from West Germany, and it delivered less sound effects than the speaker box I made. There were two thing that were clear: my Mom loves me and love is blind. This was the proof.

The boys could not master darkroom technology, but we could all do it when we were ten years or older. During the Tiananmen Square protest in June 1989, this skill became very important. It became the most powerful weapon to crack the Chinese Communist party's lies in their propaganda at that time.

Printed and corroded electronical circuit board. Painting and corrosion, a bit of a chemical taste. This was my favourite. I went into downtown Beijing City. In between XiSi and Xidan there is a second-hand electronic equipment and parts store to buy a piece of copper-coated electric isolation board, 0.50/2-inch square, very expensive, eh? Take it home and draw a circuit diagram on the copper plate to cover it under the paint so that the copper underneath does not meet the iron trichloride solution that corrodes the copper. Where's this iron trichloride going? A child of a chemist knows this. And that is me, I am more spiritual in this regard. Know that iron trichloride is a fast-drying cement reagent. The bunker construction sites must use this.

Then Steel Courtyard was my parents university. Its full name was the Peking Institute of Iron and Steel Industry; "Steel Courtyard" for short. I will mention it again and again. The Steel Courtyard had a Family Ding compound, the headquarters of bunker construction. They must have had the stuff I needed, the yellowish-green liquid. I stole a porcelain bowl from my home (not in a metal container with a liquid that corroded the metal, which I also know!) and filled it half full with that chemical and brought it home. I soaked the painted circuit board and put it on a coal stove and cooked it up. The copper plate, which is not covered with paint, gradually decays, disappears, and the solution turns black and dark green. I did it at home. The bottom of the bowl is permanently coated with blue matter and can no longer be used as a food container. Is that blue colour China blue or Dutch blue? I am not sure. I pretended to break the bowl and got a few scolds. Using this homemade printed circuit board, I made a single-tube radio. To prove that I made it myself, here's a special list of parts and their prices:

- Magnetic rod: 0.30 yuan/6 cm
- Paint-clad copper coils, homemade, didn't pay

- Single-link variable capacitor for switching broadcast stations: 1.05 yuan
- Three-foot PNP Ge-transistor: 0.10 yuan only (single-tube refers to this, an amplification transistor)
- Diode: 0.5 yuan by two
- Several capacitors: resistors are cheap, less than 0.07 yuan each
- Variable resistance: 0.20/each, with volume adjustment
- Headphones: 2.11 yuan each. Because the single tube simply does not drive the smallest loudspeaker, it can only be used with a headset to listen to its amplified sound. After all, the sound is not loud.

The headphone jack was 0.78 each: too expensive. I made it by myself at home, so it was free.

Used this transistor radio I followed the Beijing official broadcasting English course for years.

By 1988, there was no commercial karaoke machines on the market, but there was already a video screening hall or mini theater, 0.3–0.5 yuan per person, showing

Hong Kong martial arts films, Japanese TV series or the 007 series. James Bond was particularly popular with the general audience, but they did not understand him. It doesn't matter if you didn't understand, there was me. I was an unofficial English–Chinese interpreter; I could deal with four or five foreign language speakers at the same time then, and now I use the unit's video player. Equipped with a homemade microphone, I acted as a projectionist, an oral translator, plus a voice actor; I simulated a female voice in a moment, and then an old man's the next. In those evenings to late nights, there was nowhere to find night life in the largest city in China except for my place. I turned my daytime working place into a night club in the nighttime. There one could play ping-pong and bridge—a card game that became popular because the great leader and economic reform designer and engineer Mr. Deng Xiao Ping liked to play cards this way. Last but not least, I played the latest version of a James Bond movie. All businessmen on trips to Beijing, regardless of what they do in the daytime, spent the nighttime with me in my place, because they got in for free. Mostly they were coal mine engineers and technical cadres. I was, too. I could do this all night.

My hard work and my best service brought about unexpectedly good results: I went on business trips to the coal mine almost biweekly. Once I had met the people I had entertained with screenings of foreign videos in Beijing, their business trips would be successfully completed, so were mine. I did not necessarily recognize them and have active contact with them first, but they all knew me and took the initiative to recognize each other. Working like this, it doesn't bother anyone, and I don't need to play by a hidden rule—you don't have to go in through the back door. I seem to be either very decent or close to a conflict of interest. This kind of relationship is unusual and priceless.

As for what I can do, after all? I list them all below:

- Homemade Speaker box
- TV accompaniment
- Single-tube, medium-wave amplitude transistor radio
- Ore radio
- Headphone socket
- Electric solder
- Black-and-white film processing

- Film-to-photo development
- With a choice of at least with two font styles, I could write slogans, banners, contours
- Photography
- Video recording with a camcorder
- Video recorder transcription
- TV program downloading
- Translation of foreign TV films
- Bicycle repairs
- Car repairs
- Ship repair and shipbuilding
- Welding
- Electrician
- Plumbing
- Chinese food cooking
- Newspaper and magazine editing
- Composition
- Letter writing
- Good Chinese English
- Bike/tricycle riding
- Car/truck/motorboat/forklift driving

As for being an official? Business? Not me.

4
Shovel Snow

Shovelling snow is a cost-free job. At the beginning of 1987, Harbin encountered a big snowstorm. Commuter cars could not drive. The whole city, from the Harbin City Communist party chief down to ordinary agency staff, all came together in the street with shovels to dig their city out from about one metre of snow. An hour later the road was clear; all downtown roads were free of snow and ice. It was all done.

What's a commuter car? Larger institutes had one to two buses to do internal shuttle bus service only. Usually, departure time was Monday through Saturday morning at about 6:30, and they would drive along the prescribed route, stop at the prescribed pick-up station, open the doors, pick up their institute employees and take them to work. Every afternoon at 5:00 the shuttle buses were sent out again, driving along the prescribed route, stopping at the drop-off station, opening the door, bringing the institute employees home from work. This is a kind of welfare, called "commuter car," and the official worship director, the deputy director, also "enjoyed" this benefit in order to be friendly. They did not use special luxury cars to commute. Ministers had better benefits. They would no longer ride in a commuter car. They all had full-time drivers paid for by affiliated institutes for each minister and deputy minister. They had a luxury car for each minister and deputy minister, paid for by affiliated institutes too. As ministers or deputies, they did not have to pay a cent! They didn't even pay for gas. Sometimes the driver was late, so he or she had to perform a reflection in writing and read it aloud at some kind of meeting. Tough job, eh? That is to say, the model of his/her car directly marked the ranking of his/her passenger. Old models like domestic Shanghai six-cylinders, imported Volgas, joint-venture VW Santanas, German Audi 100s, Japanese Toyota Crown super sedans, Nissan Blue Birds, etc. If you saw these cars on the road at that time (1975-1989), you knew there was an officer of minister ranking on his way. Generals were not happy. They wanted to ride luxury cars too. Senior generals made them happy by importing hundreds of Mercedes-Benzes directly from Germany and smuggling them all using a warship!

I worked in an institute. Its head had a higher ranking—say, eighth–so he enjoyed a Mercedes-Benz 220 in the 1960s. The car was beige, the body was heavy, and the door banged, shocking the nearby people. Officers make people scared of them. This is a kind of Chinese tradition, which is still in effect today. Chinese officers are so illegally powerful. They can put anybody under custody, bring him to jail, torture him without going through the legal ways.

Unlike today's Ferraris or Rolls-Royces, at that time expensive cars were rare. The average person wanted to buy a bicycle and one out of one hundred could not get one—they didn't have the stamps. They had to roll dice to get good luck to buy a bicycle. One simply couldn't buy a bike without such a stamp. Why should they talk about cars and private cars?

I first rode in a Mercedes-Benz S300 in 1990, in Mercedes-Benz's hometown: Stuttgart, Germany. Adam Shall, German Chinese Association president to Aachen and Helmut Deal had such a car. And his wife Christl

Deal was the driver. I will tell stories about them later in special chapters. Decades later, in 2008, when I drove my own Mercedes, the feeling of wellbeing from riding a Mercedes-Benz was no longer there. Is it because there are more cars, or is it because the 1990s Mercedes joint-ventured with Chrysler swapped their massive parts for the later smaller ones? Anyway, Mercedes does not make a banging sound when its doors close, but another cheap sound. Even Mercedes' iconic dual horn had been sold to Toyota, but they left GM's mono-horn. Chinese folksinger Li Shuangjiang became TV joker Pan Changjiang. The metallic voice has been changed. This is just an example.

Oh! I must return to telling the snow-shovelling story. When I was young kid, the snow in Beijing city could be heavy. Once, after the snow, my "little elder brother" hung out with me at the Beihai Park, or North Sea Park, to have a snowball fight. We rolled downhill from the top of the artificial mountain. My entire body was submerged in snow! As a six-year-old little stinky boy I had a tenacious resistance to my cousin. He is seven or eight years older than I am. He's aggressive. I struggled in my defense; both of us were happy. The air at that time had no air-quality issue at all. It was so fresh, so oxygen-rich in the North Sea Park, in the centre of Beijing City.

In the winter season in 1984, I had a last snowball fight with my schoolmates from the Beijing Graduate School of the China University of Mining Technology on the ice of Kunming Lake in the Summer Palace, a park in west suburban Beijing.

In 1995 my first job in Canada was driving a snowplough truck in Toronto. My boss, a Chinese visa student at the University of Toronto, Mr. Zhao Jun, paid me $800/month, while an ordinary city worker as a snowplough driver was paid $40/hour. They worked two days to make the same amount of money that I, as a new immigrant, had to work a whole month to make, regardless of whether it was dark, a weekend or a holiday. If there was snow, I had to be in action. Christmas Eve in 1995 was a snow day in Toronto. That is an everlasting memory.

In the wintertime of 2012/13, I drove a snowplough again. This time I cleared driveway and parking-lot snow for the Passmore Badminton clubhouse in Scarborough, Ontario. Thank God I gave up on time. My landlord Jackie Chan (he was from Vietnam, he wasn't the international movie star) called a stop to my contract with the property management under his daughter Jeremy, and he hired another professional landscaping/snow removal man for half price, which was $2000/month. Poor old man. In just a month, heavy snow hit Toronto. He could not handle it anymore and gave up too. My landlord Jackie had to contract a dozer and bobcat heavy-duty-machinery-equipped company to remove the snow from his land for $1000/hour! The snow hills piled up to three stories high, and they did not melt completely until June the next year.

Now kids are still playing in the snow, but in other ways. They go to ski resorts. They play with snowboards too. They wear pairs of anti-snow-blind sunglasses, as well as polarized sunglasses—how much money is that? I never heard of it when I was young. Blue Mountain in Ontario, Canada has world-class skiing resorts. My only child, my daughter Christl Cheng, learned her skiing ABCs there. Note, please, that her name is also Christl. I named her after Christl Deal, the Czech/German lady I mentioned above.

All right, let's come back again and continue our snow-shovel stories. Snow from the roof and the coal stove burning, the condensation was dripping from the chimney, the snow was melting along the eaves of the old house, flowing to the ground. The ice formed a small sloped hillside, which was slippery. Stepping onto it, it was inevitable that one would accidently fall. One of our children's household chores was to eradicate this ice path. -20°C was the typical temperature in Beijing in the winters of my childhood. We used a knife, but it didn't help much to remove the ice. Very often the knife only made a mark on the ice. Let's change our tool from a knife to an axe. We had to make sure our axe would not crack the bricks underneath. I had never heard of anyone spreading salts. Too luxurious? The house was warmed with a coal-burning stove. In the wintertime it never extinguished, the outside of the furnace was covered in barbed wire, or tin net, because the single-layer casting iron body of the stove was very close to the bed. This could set the entire house on fire. Protective barbed wire or iron-plate fence was a must. Washed socks, shoe pads, and clothes were hung on it. Was there underwear? No, it was a kind of close-fitting tweezer, the kind of clothes that can be worn directly in the summer, somewhat like a sleeveless T-shirt or a vest with holes in its sides, to save things. The complexity of the clothes and their evolution all the way toward Canada Goose, etc. … these historical developments will be in chapters in the future. Here, removing moisture from shoes and clothes was the priority. Where was Prada, Nike, Adidas? Those were fashion only. They were useless in fighting against low temperatures in the wintertime. There was only cotton stuff. What was good was that white plastic or car tires were the basic materials. This was a kind of cotton shoe; with shoelaces they were more advanced. No-shoelace shoes were called "bean-paste burger shoes." For old men they were fine. For children, wearing such shoes would cause laughter, discrimination. Homemade shoes were often "bean-paste burger shoes," or "old man shoes." The pants' lower end had to be stuffed into socks or banded tightly, otherwise snow and ice poured in—that is cold, eh? My family was so-called "rich"; that is, there were socks I could exchange—wash this pair while wearing the other. Kids from poor families could not afford to exchange socks every day. The smells tell you the difference. Some good years I could afford to wear nylon socks, which were more stinky. But they are colourful, fashionable, and elastic. Mind you, they stink. "Smelly beauty" was the popular expression at that time, and richer people have wool socks.

Their kids wear cotton socks on their feet, with nylon socks on top as fashion. Put on a layer of stitched wool socks; now that is warm. I had only one pair. I did not understand how to maintain or take care of them. I wore them to play football, to kick the ice and rocks. After a month or so my toes came out of them and I couldn't wear them any longer. Frozen toes cause itching. The heel tendon above the foot became a large area of rough skin from the frozen spring: frozen, cracked. Today, children do not have such painful experiences. At that time, we all had this, rich and poor, adult or child. And we suffered.

There was a wonderful thing in my childhood: I had a delicate copper pot, called "hot water pot," and rubber products called "warm water bags" or "thermals." On every cold night they warmed my cold feet so that I could fall asleep. My grandmother made a cloth wrapping for the copper pot to prevent the hot water from burning my feet. That was the kind of spoiling I could feel. My grandmother had many grandsons, though not every grandchild had a pot. All my cousins who were older than me didn't have one, so how did they beat the cold and get up every morning? What did they do before bedtime? Did they bathe their feet with hot water? I never considered it. There was no fresh-water supply in the room, and of course there was no toilet, either. Brush your teeth every morning, wash your face and feet at night, cold water or hot water? I really don't know! I was scrubbed with a hot towel—scrubbed with soap, anyway.

I didn't live with my parents for the first six years of my life, but with my grandparents. Every weekend, or biweekly weekends, my father picked me up and took me, the little guy who's smelly, to the public bathroom, or the place called the bathhouse. It has a popular name today: spa. 0.26 yuan per head; good service, despite it being expensive. The average price to take a bath in a public bathhouse is 0.05 yuan per head. My bathhouse was Beijing's famous Huaqing Spa; it was located on Wangfujing Street, the most famous commercial street in Beijing, perhaps also in China, for that matter. From my grandmother's home it was walking distance. Everyone undressed, put his clothes into his locker. He got a key to that locker for the day. The locker was right beside his bed. There was also a little table at his bedside. 0.26 yuan also includes a bedspread, unlimited towel exchange, dry or hot and wet ones for different courses, and hot bathwater and adjustable warm shower water. From the change room, we would go into a huge bathroom attached to the shower room. We'd take a bath first; there was three pre-set temperatures, and the big bathtub could take ten to twenty people at the same time. You would be rubbing your own skin and others'. This was the most meaningful action from the spa or bath in the world. I guess that is why we needed to bathe together. The rest of the world prefers to bathe alone, shower alone. They do not need this rubbing. They spend extra money to get a body massage, or body rub, in short. Later, I went to a bathroom with my elder cousin, and I could not recall these feelings of wellbeing. Why? Was the massage poor in quality? Or was the towel and bed service gone? There's no way to talk about it: my cousin Zhang Weiqing and I performed back massages on each other and that is the only memory, everything else I forget.

In 2016 in Shanghai, Mu Jun, my classmate from elementary school all the way to university studies, and I had another experience in a bathhouse. I had almost no feeling at all. Back to Beijing, Wei YouZhi, my schoolmate at a graduate school, experienced another time. No memories were recalled. I even went to a luxurious bathhouse with a free buffet and drinks—soft drinks and beers and wines—with a few female classmates of mine. There was not that feeling I just described. People! Bitter experiences cannot be forgotten, but sweet ones are often forgotten. In 2016 in Tokyo, Japan, Wang Xiaodong and I experienced a Japanese-style bathhouse. In 2016 in LiYang, all my schoolmates from the graduate school experienced an open-air thermal-spring water bath. In 2003 in Frankfurt and Mainz, I experienced many Romanesque baths, Rhein-Mainz thermal ones. Can you say that I am a lucky guy? I am.

My bath stories are continuous. In 1987 in Xi'an LinYi Huaqing pool, I was on my honeymoon and it was interrupted by an emergency call—the American Department of Energy director John A. Herbst was in China. His was unhappy with his interpreter, Mr. Liu XiaoMing. He wanted me. I had served him as an interpreter in 1985 and 1986. Back to my bath journal. I have also been to the Grand Hotel in the Netherlands. I have been in an outdoor bath place in Canada's Blue Mountain Ski Resort. You name places, I have been there bathing. Is it bragging?

In 1995 when I first arrived in Canada, I couldn't find a job, so I worked in a background role for my movie idol

Chou Yun-Fat, known as "Brother Fat." An image of me taking a bath in substitution of Brother Fat was on the screen for Mr. Zhou's Hollywood movie *The Corrupters*. After the cameras rolled, it was about dinner time. Brother Fat appreciated all the crew members, including me. His appreciation was splendid. Everybody got a half piece of Boston lobster, about a pound in weight, as the main course, such a large potion that it made everybody happy. We loved him more than ever.

This chapter begins with shovelling snow and ends with all kind of baths. Is it a lifestyle, a way of thinking, or ethics of behavior? You will understand in your way.

5

Kitchen Knife or Axe

Is a kitchen knife a cold weapon or just kitchenware? I can't decide. the People's Republic of China has had ten top marshals in its seventy-year history. Marshal He Long was in the top five. In his youth he had two axes with him to rob official salt dealers and merchants. He did so not just for money but to challenge the power. In 1920s China, salt was not only expensive, but also exclusively dealt by the government. Like tobacco and alcohol, salts were the government's monopoly. With his two axes He Long robbed salt dealers, got the salt, and exchanged it for money. With the money He Long replaced his cold weapon, the axe, with hot weapons: guns. If you had a gun, you were a real anti-government armed force. Somehow, He Long was brainwashed. He accepted the Communist ideas. "The core strength of the bandits is the Communist party of China, and the theoretical basis of the idea of guiding us robins to break the law is Marxism-Leninism." These are Mao Zedong's original words. The Red Army concurred all over the country in 1949 and founded a so-called central government of the People's Republic of China. Soon after that, they rated some military officers, who supported him with more soldiers and troops, and he was not killed by internal (within the Chinese Communist party) and external (the Chinese National party) enemies, nor killed by the domestic (Chinese minorities) and international (Russian and Japanese) enemies. He Long was ranked in the top ten. Ten Marshals were born then. This piece of history is the favourite of any boy's inspirational stories: a peasant with two axes becomes a marshal.

The first time I saw the revolution with an axe in my eyes was when I was six. I was in my apartment in 1966 at the beginning stage of the Cultural Revolution. The Red Guards were popular within universities, middle schools and even elementary schools, and red army soldiers illegally hunted counter revolutionaries everywhere. Teachers, deans, principals and even classmates were victims. What a terrorist attack it was! Victims were illegally arrested, illegally tortured, illegally publicly abused, illegally prosecuted to death. Gunning down victims was the mildest way to kill them.

One night, a group of people came to my apartment building, the teachers' residence #7 building, unit 309. My neighbour in unit 310 foresaw getting into "bloody trouble." Mr. Chen Fang, my next-door neighbour, was the director of the university library. At that time, his Beijing Iron and Steel Institute library was ranked the fourth largest collection in Beijing. The top three were the Beijing National Library, Peking University Library and Beijing Teachers' University Library. Director Chen's household of four lived in 310, a three-bedroom apartment. He wouldn't open the door at the violent knock.

This group of people were college students or college graduates—we called them "the Axes"—and among them was one with the character of a gangster. His scientific studies did not diminish his gangster character at all, even though his studies and others acknowledging him should have made it so. He was copying Marshal He Long. They did not go back to ask their leaders; they did not take a written house-search warrant or an arrest warrant to carry out the arrest of Director Chen. There were no such things issued at all. They immediately turned around and knocked on my apartment door, unit 309. We opened the door fearfully. They wanted to borrow an axe. My apartment had only a light kitchen knife and my parents lent it to them. One of them, the one I mentioned just now, wanted to show the revolutionaries how to begin a revolution. He copied Marshal He Long and chopped the door of unit 310 until the door was broken, cut it open, and Director Chen was caught in front of his wife and their two teenage sons. The young boys were sixteen and fourteen years old. Our kitchen knife was in bad shape when it was returned to us. We did not complain. Who dares? Director Chen Fang had two sons, their nicknames were Dafei and Erfei, which means they were fat boy #1 and #2. Although they were older than I was but not strong enough to challenge the coup, which took their dad into custody in a brutal way. After this horrible night no one could see them again. I heard that they went to the countryside and became farmers. The latest information tells that fat boy #1 became a professor of instant noodle processing. His counteraction against the ex-premier Li Peng at his official funeral service in Beijing on July 29,

2019 resulted in his arrest. He is now famous in China, and his name is Chen Zhao Zhi.

Soon, Family Chen was forced to vacate two of the three bedrooms in apartment 310 and another family moved in with three sons. Their parents were logistics workers in the university. Director Chen was publicly humiliated (it was not a public trial) in an all-staff general meeting at the track and field playground in the university. Thousands of people saw Director Chen, together with two or three other victims, placed on benches, bent over by two young revolutionaries by pulling their arms backward and upright in the air. The victims' hair was pulled backwards so that they had to face the audience. There were big signs hanging on their necks with their own name marked with a red cross, and the brief crime was added to the sign by the Axes. Director Chen attempted suicide, shamed after this humiliation. Nobody would mention him again. They are all still in China and they all fear the Axes. I'm outside of China now. I can speak and write freely. I can recall and record some historical facts in as much detail as I can. If I don't write these here, if you don't read them from here, maybe this piece of history will be lost forever.

How terrible the Cultural Revolution was. No event or social movement should last as long as ten years, so widely as to affect each corner of social life, so deeply maiming people that they have to lie or cover whatever they had done during the revolution, chopped or been chopped, damaged or maimed. What happened on Earth is not one conclusion—a few books or a museum can tell the following generations clearly. Because of that, the chopper-holders or Axes are still in power. They are the power. Then there are truths. I believe truths will soon be disclosed.

For about year or so, it was my father's turn. Instead of being arrested from his home, he was taken away from his desk at the physics and chemistry faculty. He was taken under custody illegally in a room of the student dormitory building #12 with a wooden board nailed on its only window to make it impossible to see through. Why should I use the word "illegally" again and again? See these facts:

- The Axes were not policemen and they imprisoned innocent people.
- The student room in the university campus is not a prison and they, the Axes, turned it into one.

- My father and other victims, including Director Chen, were not sentenced to stay in the "jail," and the Axes said their "sentencing" was more powerful than the courts.

The sub-movement in the Cultural Revolution hit him. This sub-movement was called a "clean-up troops action." My father was cleared out of the ranks of the revolutionary class by the Axes with an excuse: under suspicion of being KMT (the Chinese National party) agents, the worst crime one could imagine at that time, simply because KMT beat the last dynasty, The Qing Dynasty, which came to power all over China in 1905 ahead of the Chinese Communist party, who took it over from KMT in 1949. The CCP paid tens of thousands of lives in the civil war against the KMT.

After the end of the Cultural Revolution, at my father's high school reunion, all the survivors found that they, including several who had passed away, were all hit with this KMT agent suspicion. They were the unlucky ones. The source/root cause was one classmate who was a member of a Kuomintang youth organization called the "Three Youth Leagues" who was exposed at the Cultural Revolution, beaten and tortured. When he really could not suffer any more, he turned himself over to the Axes and said that the whole class were members of the Kuomintang Three Youth Leagues. Every one of his classmates, including my father, were arrested and tortured by the Axes. The same thing happened to everybody; no one could bear the brutal and disgraceful tortures and they all surrendered. They all told the Axes the same story: all classmates were KMT. The Axes wanted to arrest and torture more people to fulfill themselves by doing all their criminal things free from punishment or anyone fighting back, and to delight their great leader, Mao. But a class had so few students that they were all exposed, and each person exposed others. This game went into a dead cycle.

On that day, my mother, Shen FengYun, had just a few minutes to prepare a toothbrush and laundry for my dad, Cheng ShuWu, and she handed them over to the Axes, who ordered my dad to the jail and ordered my mom to be quiet. At that time, my mother was pregnant. My younger brother had only been in her tummy for a few weeks. My father was jailed on the campus of the very university that my mom and dad worked for, the Beijing University of Science and Technology, formerly and originally the Institute of Iron and Steel Industry, Peking. We and others call it by its nickname, "the Steel Courtyard," a place we knew very well, and we knew where the Axes jailed my dad but they did not allow us to visit him.

In the middle of a dark and windy night, two Axes crept into my apartment—my family of four or five had only one bedroom in that apartment, #309—to terrify my mother, a Shanghai Fudan University graduate student and young female teacher in Beijing lecturing at the Faculty of Math, Physics, Chemistry, and Foreign Languages. She was one of very few female teachers in an engineering school at that time. My father was not home but in the jail the Axes created, and they further used this opportunity to assault my mother. My sister Cheng Jie and I were sleeping. I was woken up by my mom's sobbing. I dared not make any noise nor move to attract the Axes' attention, but lay shivering in my quilt. I'm such a useless thing—the only man in that bedroom in that time who failed to stand up, the other two in our bedroom were Axes! Pigs!

The Axes entered another house full of people one night, and the husband in that house was not in but had been put away by the Axes. They also knew that this was evil. They made no noise this time, unlike other days when they showed up and made enormous amounts of noise, yelling, shouting, reading Mao's instructions loudly. These things made my mother sick. She could not peacefully rest to assure that the baby in her tummy was fine. My younger brother was not fine. He got shocks, too, during my mom's pregnancy, before he was born in February 1969. My younger brother Cheng Xuan suffers from a heart disorder from his birth. We all blame the Axes.

All this happened on the campus of a contemporary university, an engineering school of technical civilization. Originally an engineering student uses his/her brain only to contribute his/her knowledge to secure his/her community, and to make sure its members live a better and safer life. In the time of the Cultural Revolution, students, include engineering students and others, put on a piece of red ribbon with a golden-coloured "Red Guard" on it, becoming devils immediately. They cracked the legal system. The cracked the government. They kicked out officers. They cracked schools. At temples they cracked Buddhas. At private homes they cracked furniture, paintings, kitchenware, quality cloths, high heels, leather shoes, furs, silks, makeup stuff. The worst thing they did was destroy everybody's dignity. It makes everyone feel that in such a crowd of gangsters you are nothing. You can live a miserable life only, apply and get subsidies, and welfare is the greatest honour. Why did my dad and Director Chen get such unfair humiliations? They were just slightly richer in the brain. Mao did not like this and wouldn't allow anybody to be smarter than he was. His followers delighted him by doing all kinds of bad things against these "rich men." The way the Axes tortured my dad was to grab his hair, shake him back and forth and smash his head into the steel rack of his bunk bed. They wanted my dad to lose his intelligence from this maiming.

The most perverted thing is that there was a female version of the Axes' brutality. She graduated from the University of Iron and Steel and stayed and worked at the same university as a teaching assistant. Lady Wang. She tortured a male lecturer, Luo JingYuan, who graduated from Fudan University in Shanghai. Everything was the same as with my mom, before and after coming to Beijing. Uncle Luo was also a chemist. Lady Wang tortured him by using her bare hands to pull out his chest hair! Uncle Luo had some chest hair. This is rare in Sino-national people. They do not all have this hair. Is this what caught the Axes' attention, and they were suspicious of foreign blood in Uncle Luo's body? From the Axes' point of view, their "class struggling point of view," it is a born crime, or as you guys call it, "the original one." And she, the Lady Wang, pulled out a few hairs from Uncle Luo's chest one after another.

Attention Axes: once China has real legal systems following the rest of the world, and don't have the Chinese way of additives or moderates in them, I will sue you. Make sure all you Axes are still alive by that time. I, Bill Cheng Xun, must stand up to sue the Axes, and send you to the rule-of-law standardized jails one after another!

Outside of schools and university campuses, the situation was even more uncivilized. My grandparents lived in a small courtyard in Beijing, and they had no power. If you looked at the two stone carvings at the gate of the courtyard, it was a pair of dogs, not a pair of lions nor Kirin, etc.—high-level fictional animal statues that do not actually exist in China. After studying the stone carvings on the doorstep of the courtyard, it was found that the courtyard was the safeguard's home. The stone dogs secure the door of the safeguard's house, and the safeguard secures the emperor's palace, the Forbidden City in Beijing. My grandfather came to Beijing from Province Shandong in the 1920s. The Emperor was long gone since the revolution led by Dr. Sun Yat-Sen in 1905, and the safeguard had run away from his home in Beijing. His courtyard was empty. Beijing was not the capital city in China from 1905 to 1949, but Nanking. Somehow my grandpa, the "number seven master"—people called him this and he enjoyed it—obtained the courtyard. And his role in Beijing coincidently was the same as the safeguard to the Emperor: a policeman.

It could be that my grandpa's brother-in-law had power, the bureau director of the Beijing-Hankou railway. The brother-in-law had several houses in Beijing, of course. I know he had two houses nearby my grandparent's house in Beijing. Within our families we call them east courtyard and west courtyard for each of his sons, Wang Xu Qin and Wang Xu Zao. Along with my grandparent's courtyard, the three houses are together in the same hutong in Beijing. At the beginning of the Cultural Revolution, a group of people rushed in, announcing the occupation.

The entire house was searched. All furniture was removed to the open-air part of the courtyard house; the interior courtyard was in an upside-down way. I was only six years old and I rushed away to the west courtyard. There the situation was not good, either. Several days prior, it had been robbed. All the furniture was taken. The west courtyard was almost empty. I did not see the robbery in process, but I suffered, too. It changed my life. The Axes disappointed this time, probably because my grandpa had nothing valuable. His home had decayed, there was no quality furniture, no antiques nor paintings in the house. He was an enlightened man who sent all his children to church schools, private schools, the best middle school in Peking. Boys went to Yu Ying Boys' School (founded in 1864 by an American), while girls went to Bridgeman Girls' School (founded in 1864 by American). Then they went to Tsinghua, which advocated the European/American way of studies.

My grandma, "the Seventh Lady," spent all her savings and sold all her jewelry before the Chinese Communist party and its Red Army took over Beijing in a peaceful way in 1948, to support her sons and daughters so they could study in modern schools. She could read and write.

It meant that she, as a girl in the last dynasty, was able to go to school. If it was not a public school, it must be a private school/private tutor for rich families called "SiShu." All right. The Red Guards didn't find anything counter-revolutionary, so they kicked out my grandmother Guo ShuZhen—we all called her NaiNai—my other grandma Zhang Zaizhi—we all call her HaoNaiNai, which is "Nice Granny"—my aunt number one, Cheng ShuShun, and two of her sons; my cousin Sa BenJie—he just passed away on August 8, 2019 at his age of 71; he has no nickname—and Sa BenRen, whose nickname is "the Little"; my grandfather's number-one grandson, my cousin Cheng Peng—his nickname is DengDeng (in the 1980s he changed his name and family name to Wei Ran to show his respect to his mother, the nation-wide famous actress ShangGuan YunZhu. She took her own life during the Cultural Revolution to prove that she was innocent and did not tease the greatest leader Chairman Mao); and me, Bill Cheng Xun—my nickname is the best of them all: YueLiang, which is "the Moon." They kicked us all out from that courtyard. My Grandma cried and told my Dad: "The axes are wild dogs!" My dad covered his mom's mouth. Thank God no one was nearby. We seven became homeless. Six people out of seven had no jobs, no income, no place to stay overnight. Four boys were too young to work, and two grannies were too old to work. Three other family members—my grandfather, my other grandma and their only granddaughter, my female cousin #1 Cheng Gong—her nickname is LinLin—were left over to live in a small room in the west row of that courtyard. The other three better rows of buildings—say the east, north and south ones—were forced to rent out to several tenants by the so-called "bureau of house and property management." They did not have any properties. We did. And what's more important is that we did not contract them to run our properties and houses. It was pure robbery! They were as qualified as the Axes. I make no mistakes. There was no lease agreement between a landlord and the tenants without paying rent not to the landlord but to the "bureau."

I remember there was a Family Liu of five people and a Family Guo of five people. Both families moved into our north row house, where it was the best quality, and normally the highest-ranked people of a family lived there in Chinese tradition. South house, east house and the concierge room were all occupied by unknown people. I cannot recall any of them. The tenants paid so-called rent to the "bureau" symbolically. It was worse than if they did not pay rent at all. That "rent" meant the bureau had the property and assigned it to its favourite Axes. It turned an illegal occupancy into a legal one. Besides, the rent was so low it could not cover maintenance, repairs for the house. It was even less than the utility bill.

I believe in the proverb "when a door closes a window opens." It indeed happened to us poor homeless people! This time it was my aunt number one, Cheng ShuShun. She had a job as an accountant her whole life. Her institute was the Central Orchestra Musical Band. The band moved from Donghuamen, in the Dongcheng district of the Beijing city core within the first circle in Beijing, to the north-easterly Chaoyang District, the third concentric circle in Beijing. My aunt was able to rent two bedrooms from a three-bedroom unit in a very high-quality apartment building. There was a warm-water radiator in each bedroom; one lovely bedroom faced south and a smaller one faced north, and there was a kitchen with water and sink and a two-flame gas stove, a sit-in toilet with flush, and a balcony facing north. My aunt took all the homeless people in my large family to live here.

From the end of the 1960s to the early 1980s, it became our family's meeting place. Usually my cousin squeezed into the small north bedroom and my two grandmothers and my aunt squeezed into the big south bedroom. It was meaningful to all three old women. They needed sunshine the most.

On New Year's Day, the lunar one, the family of more than twenty sat here around two tables to celebrate. Adults were in the south bedroom and children were in the north bedroom for a very good meal that we could only dream about on the rest of the days of the year. I'm my grandmother's first grandson, so she, the highest ranked one in the house, personally arranged for me to sit at the adults' table once. In the 1970s, I passed 25 yuan a month on my dad's behalf to my grandmother. China has had this tradition for many years, many generations. Elder people did not get any government funding, any retirement payments whatsoever, except from their children.

I rode a bicycle and spent an hour or so crossing about 20 km from my parents' home to this house. My school report had a proud showtime in there. I lay next to my grandma; she was disabled and almost blind in her last several years. She stayed in her bed all day long. I told her my school performance and scores. Physical: 100, full marks, chemistry: 99.5—pity, I failed to add a slash in naming an organic compound, and that slash cost me -0.5 point—math: 100, full marks also. These are the three majors. Even my grandma knew. Other subjects were nothing, but I'd liked to show my grandma to make her happy. I was a good student. English: 95, OK, politics: 97 percent, Chinese: 98.5, ranking the class number one that school year. Awards? "Three good students." This title only went to those ranked top three in a class, and each class had more than fifty students. Soon it was 1977, the national high school educational entrance examination, 1 percent of the candidates from the whole country could go to universities. I wrote the exams. The Chinese language: 79 points (100 is the full mark), math: 67 points, physics plus chemistry: 66 points, politics: 71 points, altogether I got 283 points, exceeding the Beijing qualification score line, which was 260. Although I got 23 points higher, eh? But still I was not able to go to university. Here again the laws played no roles, they were just policy. Universities admitted candidates at large at the 260 line and admitted school students at another line, which was 280 and above.

I was a student of Grade 10. According to my school principal Mrs. Zhang Yu Ting, I should have continued my studies at her high school. Double standard. Ha. My grandma was disappointed. And she left the world for another lifetime. It was all my fault. I was not allowed to write the state university entrance exams until 1979, before I went to college.

In the early 1980s, my little elder cousin Sa Benren got married and raised his only son, Sa Long. In the mid-1980s, my number two aunt Cheng Shuqi's daughter, my #3 female cousin Liu Ye, transferred to Beijing from Shanxi Province Huo County, completed her high school courses and national college entrance exams in the kitchen of that apartment, and entered the Beijing United University. It's here too that my "nice grandma" gave me love and marriage guidance. I was nervous chasing a pretty schoolmate of mine. Her dad was a university professor. "Don't hesitate to marry her. Your dad is also a university professor." My grandma's words made up my mind. Here, my aunt #1 gave me occupational guidance and even ordered me to stay at the same school after my post-study. My elder cousins took turns guiding me to play violin, to write brush-paintings, to read famous writers' works/books and in my spare time to self-study tuition materials. This apartment was a blessing for the younger generation. Our common elder generations, two grandmas and my eldest aunt, never went back to that inauspicious old courtyard. They passed away peacefully in that apartment.

At the beginning of the Cultural Revolution, when Axes attacked our homes, my aunt from my mother's side Shen Fengqin's home in the eastern suburbs of Beijing was also attacked by the brutal Axes. They suspected that my aunt might have gold bars in the mezzanine at the top of the wooden double bed, so he chopped it with his actual axe and split the bed completely. There was nothing there. Why suspect my aunt was hiding her treasure? My aunt was an accountant at a Beijing chemical general plant before and after moving to Beijing from Shanghai, and her husband Zhang Shan Xian was the chief engineer of the factory. Their own chemical company was merged (against the private business owners' willingness in the 1950s) into a state chemical plant in Shanghai. These factors were enough for the Axes to find an excuse to chop up my aunt's bed in her bedroom. My aunt's family also lost the whole apartment and was forced to move to

Bill Xun Cheng

what was then the countryside, a small village outside the east wall of the Peking University. There was not even tap water. Villagers got a well. The toilet was also public. Three hundred villagers had only one well, one toilet.

Use an axe to chop off the doors of a house, go in and kidnap the residents. Now to count, what crime should it be?

- Armed with weapons
- Gang robbery
- Hostage-taking
- Torture
- Threats to personal safety, including relatives of the suspects
- Leaving the scene after the crime
- Evicting residents from their homes
- Blocking people from visiting their relatives under custody

Any one of these crimes is enough to commit the Axe to jail for years. But in China, no one has sued to liquidate.

58

After the Cultural Revolution, my father survived. The Axes, who released him, still held the handle of the axe, and still had the right to put the axe up. They are even the same people, from the same group, and/or one of the branches of the Chinese Communist party. They told my father that it was right to catch him then, and it was right to let him go now. In other words, they reserved the right to kidnap him again at any time. My father accepted the conditions without saying anything. He had been "suspended" for so many years. The so-called suspension is not to grasp nor to judge, the suspect is not qualitative. Whenever a political movement is popping up and the atmosphere is against the suspended, he will be nominated to be criticized, and when the political movement is over and the atmosphere slightly eased, he will put aside. He isn't a target/tool/negative tutor whatsoever, but a human being. He was threatened to stay quiet, to not cause any trouble. It was hard. A university teaching staff has no independence, is not allowed to employ a creative way of thinking, has no dignity. He had to spend hours, days, weeks and months in custody, learn documents, political leaders' speeches, the People's Daily newspaper, and tell Axe that he would 100 percent support their stupid ideas and points. Political study of this kind was called "storms unmovable, thunders unbeatable" in the Cultural Revolution. It went three times a day, morning: 8:00– 12:00, afternoon: 14:00–18:00 and evenings: 19:00– 22:00, Monday through Saturday. Whoever dared to be absent or late got a huge hat thrown at his head. "Right wingers," counterrevolutionaries, etc. Each one could end his political life, and he would become a public enemy. So his relatives would be, too.

So were we children. Were we qualified to rise against the Axe? No. Including the so-called better-born workers, peasants, soldiers, and cadres, we were not allowed to form any organizations of any kind. There were a few young people who ganged up, quietly set up their own organization of an axe team, night attack teams, guerrillas, etc. A group of boys established the Jaguars. It was pulverized (cracked down on) soon after being found and reported. The Axe knew that they would pop up in this way. They always reserved power. They didn't want anybody to copy their "success" in China. Any newly formed organization would be persecuted as "organized crime," or an "illegal gang." To date, everybody knows that the Axes are the largest illegal gang in the world. It has 90 million members, and it is called "the Chinese Communist party." This gang is a perfect criminal organization because there is nowhere to find its registration.

One of the young teachers I admire is Liu Hui Guo. One day he came to my house with a sparkle in his eyes and an incomparable refinement, and a sharp sword in his arms. Unlike unearthed artifacts, the handle of the sword was tangled with copper wire or isolation-coated wire, and its gold colour shined. Coupled with the silver glitter of the blade, it was the most beautiful cold weapon I had ever seen. I took it. Well, it was a little too heavy for a child to arm himself with, but for him, a man in his twenties and thirties, such as Liu Hui Guo, a well-behaved and handsome young teacher wearing a sword to travel with, there should be unlimited beauty. Uncle Liu compared the blade to his own chest; his chest thickness was from the sword peak to the sword handle of the bracelet part. His sword could have pierced someone's chest and killed him.

A few days later came a murderous letter: youth teacher Liu Hui Guo took his own life. Today it is popular to report this death as "being suicided," which means he, among others, were killed by Axes rather than committing suicide. The causes of deaths were always a mystery—sliding, hide and seek, jumping from the top of a high building, etc. Will a good young man who loves swords commit suicide? He was the youngest one of the groups I remember who committed suicide during the Cultural Revolution. After his death, he went to his final station: an incinerator. His colleagues, schoolmates, students or the Axes did the worst things against his body, disgraceful and extremely disrespectful things. His head on the ground, dragged by his feet, his body thrown into the incinerator. This has severely affected people who commit suicide. For their own body to not be insulted, and for their dignity, they would secretly climb the iron blast furnace lime-feeding trolley, and with it rise to the top of the blast furnace where it was hotter than one thousand degrees, a huge amount of heat, and they burned to death. In doing so, even a wisp of smoke would not stay. Nothing could be left over for the Axes to insult.

What kind of humiliation is it that forces people to consider suicide? And we'll come back and tell Director Chen's story. He was dragged into the public torturing against him. His suit was not in a good shape. There was a big sign hanging from his neck by a string of cotton rope or metallic wire. His name was written in a strange way in black. On his name there was a big cross in red. He had to bend his upper body over. From the back of his body, not from the front, two Axes pulled his arms straight up. His head and his upper body leaned forward. He stood zigzag, and he had to keep the pose for longer than two hours. During this period, two of the Axes who controlled his body were rotated with the other two Axes. They switched on and off for breaks. But Director Chen did not have any breaks, not even a free hand to wipe off his tears, sweat, boogers, ugly liquids that the Axes poured onto his face. It was unbearable to see. This is called "redneck airplane." In front of more than 2,000 people, all of them knowing each other as they worked for the same university, Director Chen lost his dignity in the daytime in a crime against humanity. Events of this kind took place many times in many places in China at the beginning of the Cultural Revolution, i.e., 1966–1968.

Director Chen could not suffer. He ended his life by suicide. For some reason he didn't die. One of my schoolmates, from my elementary school to university, Mr. Ma Kun Song, saw him alive in 1977 in the very resident building where he was illegally arrested in 1967, The Cultural Revolution was over in Oct. 1976. This piece of history has been hidden. I saw this with my own eyes, these injustices from my age of six to sixteen. 43 years has been past. I should not keep them undisclosed any longer. My parents have died, I myself have been living overseas for three decades. I'm threatening Axes who are either old or dead. But my feeling of insecurity still exists. I think it's my turn to stand up and tell. I believe I am doing a good thing. If you can't have a little sense of security, then we don't deserve to have that sense of security. Axes are still there, far and close. The red Axes are all over China. And they want to spread out to the world.

Readers, I am talking about the potential threat, and that is the return of the Cultural Revolution. It is happening in China now. Suicides and being suicided is popular again in China. Mostly, politics is the root cause. Axes are torturing/killing people without hesitation.

In 1975 my dad came back to the Steel Courtyard from his place of exile. This place was among other places where government officials and schoolteachers were doing the farmer's labour jobs in the field far away from their institutions. They stayed in the camp for a year or two and were sent back to their original institutions. This is just a little better treatment than those Russian camps in

Siberia. All these places had a common name, "May 7th Carders' Camp." Mao sent his superior message about how to punish intellectuals and officials on May 7th, 1968. Axes followed their leader to set up thousands of such camps. The Chinese way of brainwashing isn't just sitting and talking, but a labour camp and imprisonment all in one.

Despite the brainwashing, my dad didn't change his mind. He found out to his surprise that some Axes became university students and were studying at his university. They named themselves "worker, peasant and soldier students." They were far away from qualifying to study at any universities. They didn't know how to study. My father joked about them by saying that they had "university signs, middle school textbooks, elementary school tuition, and kindergarten emotions." On the same day, the broadcast loudspeakers in the Steel Courtyard started the next round of verbal insults against my dad. On the same night, my home door was again knocked on by an Axe. My father answered the door; there was an actual steel kitchen knife held by one of the Axes before he entered. "Teacher Cheng, I present the knife to you. Take it!" This was one of many bad things the Axes did at the university. The Axes examined all professors using an exam sheet created by their poor brains and rich "experiences" in their daily life. This was the funniest: examination to them was equal to the hardest torture against them, while examination to professors was the easiest game; they were used to play it year after year. Axes misused their power. Such idiot "worker, peasant and soldier students" became our national leaders—chairman, general secretary, president and party chief.

Axes, you were an axe in your last lifetime. Are you an axe in this lifetime? Will you be an axe the next lifetime again and again, like forever? Are you sure?

A Buddhist believes in the cycle of lives.

A man who does all his jobs well will live his next life as a human being.

A man who did some bad things will get off from this cycle for several cycles as a non-human being and will be back as a human being again.

A man who did too many too bad things will never get a chance to live as a human being again!

Axes are the last ones. From my point of view, they do not have a chance to communicate with their successors about their lives in the other world, which are poor and sad or miserable lives as non-human beings, since they are not human being and cannot speak a language. That is why new Axes keep doing bad things. They do not know what kind of punishment is waiting for them.

Christ believes something similar, the Heaven and the Hell.

A good man goes to Heaven while a bad man goes to Hell. It is not mentioned how many times and how long each one can stay where he goes.

Interesting.

Be good …

6

Fighting, or Civil War

Below is a real war of cold weapon in China in modern times, 1967–1968. The Steel Courtyard is a Chinese copy of the Moscow Institute of Iron and Steel Industry in the ex–Soviet Union. Last century, in the early '50s, from building styles to organizational charts, we Chinese copied everything from the Russians. Long story short: Stalin, the ex-dictator, presented 600 projects to his dictatorship partner, another Dictator, Mao, for free. Among them there were universities, and the Peking Institute of Iron and Steel Industry was the top one. There will be wars and we need steel—Mao believed this. As weapon-material steel can be both a cold weapon and hot one. That is why the steelmaking was prioritized. In the Steel Courtyard, not only did people teach modern industrial technologies, iron-ore mining, extraction or processing and iron and steelmaking, but they also did steel processing, making shaving blades from stainless steel. We were good at casting, forging, spray-steelmaking, powder metallurgy, rolling, and various molding processes. Plus, welding, riveting, sawing, milling, drilling, and other ways to process/fabricate steel. Its school-run factory/workshop could manufacture knives, swords, etc.—cold weapons.

At the beginning of the Cultural Revolution, two factions of Axes prepared their own weapons and started civil wars. Which two factions did the Cultural Revolution begin to assign? The rebels and royalists. And the royalists were rebels, too. The royalty must not be shown, while their leader, the dean of the university, Mr. Gao Yun Sheng, was suicided before the faction "Commune YanAn" was organized. After a round or two of dog fights, Axes in each institute split into two factions and affiliated with each other in other institutes, and the rebels together were called the "sky faction," and the other side was automatically called the "ground faction." After the Cultural Revolution, in 1978, the former ground faction finally got a promotion. Chairman Hua Guo Feng, Mao's successor, blocked them for about two years. They were close to Deng Xiaoping in political preference. The other faction, the sky, was close to the Gang of Four, including Wang Hong Wen, VP of China, another one of Mao's successors; Jiang Qing, Mao's last wife (none of Mao's marriages were registered); another of Mao's successors, Zhang Chun Qiao, vice premier; and Yao Wen Yuan, the Chinese Goebbels, the official Chinese media chief. They were pulverized (court coup) by the last (10th) Marshall, Ye Jian Ying. Axes like this game of pulverizing each other. Dictators like this game. They were busy pulverizing their political enemies but did not even know what pulverizing meant. It means to grind cocoa beans and make them into chocolate. Chocolate makes people happy. I know it, you know it, ten nations of the world know it (Switzerland, USA, France, Belgium, the Netherlands, Canada, India, Germany, Great Britain, Japan).

I make a funny point here: the world's top ten nations know how to make chocolate, but dictators don't. As a little boy, I could only classify/judge that whoever made chocolate candies was a good guy, he who cannot is bad.

Now I will go on to talk about "wudu," or group fighting: civil wars. A student of the royalists passed away from an unknown root cause. In any kind of college and university, the tragedy should be crisis-managed by the dean, the principal. But at that time during the Cultural Revolution, even our own principal, Mr. Gao Yun Sheng, committed suicide. He used a pistol from his superiors and shot himself in his office. The timing of his suicide was perfect. He stepped away from being humiliated. But why should I call his suicide perfect? Can I use a word other than perfect? I am a Canadian now. Canadian is the nation that will say sorry for anything. I say sorry for the word "perfect." The dead student, in an industrial college or technology-concentrated university, which was built by experts from the Soviet Union in 1952, should have a more scientific and convincing account of the root cause of his death, but no. Both sides of the Axes accused the other side of killing him. They blamed each other, and both sides could not provide evidence. It was the treble of those two days. A broadcasting car repeatedly aired a ridiculous conclusion: he stepped on noodles, fell and died. "Down with the noodles!" And the other loudspeaker blared that he stepped on a cabbage leaf and fell. "Down with the cabbage!" Axes were jeopardizing his life. It was a life. My God. He was killed by Axes, and the murderer has stayed at large till today! Possibly the murderer delivers lectures at the same university. I was six years old in 1966, at most seven years old in 1967, a seven-year-old boy in the almost seventy-year war-free city of Beijing (the British and French forces invaded Beijing in the 1890s. That was the last war on record). No police enforcement could stop these crimes of killing each other. Then it was a war, a civil war.

I experienced one cold-and-hot-weapon civil war after another in the Cultural Revolution. It was scary then. It is scary now. Look at the armed students and the young teachers, they were wearing leather body armour and wicker hats, as there were no helmets at the time. The protective gear, of course, had a facemask like a fencing mask to protect with.

One day they went on parade in the resident zone of our university in the Steel Courtyard. Uniformed, with spears on their shoulders. A man posed for a photo— picture taking was OK. But a company of ancient knight-like armed soldiers marching in a peaceful residential zone was completely a message of war! We were in a civil war! And our houses nearby would become a battlefield! While marching, the student soldiers shouted: "We guard for YanAn!" Commune YanAn was the name that the Steel Courtyard loyalist named themselves. The same faction of the courtyard across the university avenue was called "the East is Red." Chinese Premier Wen Jiabao was in this group when he was a geological college student. They paraded through their battlefields and our homes, and among their homes, too. We were deadly scared. Running away home was our children's first and only reaction. We did not know that in wartime homes were unsafe but being home alive is the best in any war. Isn't it? Children knew that too; it is not jeopardized time now. Rush home close the doors and windows—we were so nervous that we almost forgot to breathe. I thought it was my last day in this world. If I made any noise, they would come to my home and kill me instantly. They didn't see me; they didn't hear me. My teeth chattered but I could not stop them. Axes broke into resident homes and grabbed people day and night during the Cultural Revolution. Who knew in advance what they were going to do next? Crazy!

Axes shaved their victims' hair and gave them a criminal look. My Chinese character tutor, famous Sinology Professor Bai Nai Zhen from Peking University, his pseudonym all his career life being Bai Hua Wen, had been a victim of this insult. The Axes shaved women's hair into a yin/yang style; that is, half of her hair was cut, leaving the other half, so that they had a ghostly look. My polymer chemistry teacher, Professor Shan Zhong Jian, suffered this insult at her age of thirty-five. Terrible. Later, in the movie Schindler's List, in a scene from the 1930s–40s, Nazi Germany suppressed and expelled Jewish people. That was one nation against another, unlike in China, where we are one nation and we kill each other. This killing had happened for ten years, from 1966–1976. Fifty years later, in 2016–2017, Beijing Mayor Cai Qi called for such an expulsion again. In this so-called "sees red blood with a bay knife action," thousands of non-Beijing residents were brutally expelled by Axes with cold weapons on a cold winter night, just one or two days before Chinese New Year, the most significant festival in China and East/Southeast Asia. Axes armed with cold weapons used their weapons to break into non-resident's temporary homes and stores, cracked furniture, stole their business devices, and beat the business owners in front of their children.

Again and again, human civilization has been trampled.

In the same year, 2017, Axes from Shanghai copied the Beijing Axes' brutal assaults. There the axes blocked all showcase windows and doors facing the street with concrete, stopping customers from entering businesses. Meanwhile, the store owners had to continue to pay their taxes, and they could not lay off clerks.

Look at our neighbor universities in 1967. We had more than ten universities along University Avenue in Beijing. There were even worse assaults. Inside the east gate of Tsinghua University, there was a modern building called the Chemistry Hall. It was burned to the ground. That was also evidence that Axes use hot weapons there in the Cultural Revolution, and the Cultural Revolution was a ten-year civil war from 1966–1976. Bulldozer-modified redneck tanks were welded with steel plates as their armour, and machine guns were mounted on top. Here it is not convenient to say that the production of Molotov cocktails was an open recipe … it would be a pure terror suspect, wouldn't it? In fact, at that time, children over the age of seven would make them DIY-style. Younger children couldn't even get empty glass bottles, so we could not make them. Battles broke out at Tsinghua University several times by people throwing Molotov cocktails and occasionally shooting guns at one another. This was stopped by the Capital Steel Corp.

Workers, Mao Zedong's thought-propaganda team. They triumphed for many years in Beijing, so from 1968 to 1976, one had better listen to what they said. And if not, Axe time! During this time of ceasefire in Beijing, they played a role as peacemakers. Holding Chairman Mao's quotes and shouting, "Long live Chairman Mao!" they successfully split into two parties of civil war partners and occupied Tsinghua University's campus. 2,000 workers were in on this action. Then began a years-long disaster—the worker's propaganda team, the military propaganda team occupied the campus, as well as the major state-owned factories, colleges and universities, taking authority over the principals, secretaries and all functional staff.

The Steel Courtyard was broken in like this, before we opened fire against anyone. The factions ceased fire and surrendered to the captain of the worker's propaganda team, Song Yong Quan, and the army representative Jin Zhao Dian. The Revolutionary Rebels commune and the YanAn commune were both dissolved. The leaders from both sides were taken into a new organization called the Revolution Committee. The substitute of governance, this action, was called "support left faction, support workers and support farmers." Since then, all kind of schools have never returned to their teaching and researching staff levels until today. The revolutionary committee had all the power. Its members or commissioners were the same groups of Axes! In other words, Axes still hold the power and employees' congresses, unions, students, scholars have no rights. Everywhere there were crises, conflicts, etc. The revolution committees and not the court gave simple but unreasonable judgement, that is revolutionary, or counter-revolutionary. Every simple tiny daily life and activity was hooked up to political preference. You want a burger? No! That is capitalism. You want to date a girl? No! That is bourgeois. You want to plant some fruit trees in your backyard? No! That is revisionism. You want to study and become smarter? No! That is counter-revolution. People believed that the more knowledge you have, the more counter-revolutionary you are. The Cultural Revolution turned everybody into an idiot. Then what could we do? Axes prohibited people from having different ideas than their own. Don't even ask what to do. Don't think. Just follow. Follow someone called the Great Guider, Great Leader, Great Marshal and Great Steersman. And that someone was Chairman Mao.

In the Steel Courtyard, the centre of power moved to the #2 building, the original college dormitory for students, later the youth teachers' residence. It was now the headquarters of the workers' Mao Ze Dong thought-propaganda team. The building was in the most convenient location: the single women's residence building, the #8 is on its east side, the domestic hospital, #3 building is on its south, and the dining hall for university staff is on its west. Get it?

From 1980 to 2003, my father had been working as a guest professor at the University Aachen in Germany for an accumulated four years. My mother had twice been to Germany, for two years altogether. My wife, Luo Ji, had been studying as a co-op doctoral candidate in Germany once for five years. I had been working as a guest engineer in Aachen Germany for six years. My daughter Christl Cheng was born in Germany and stayed there till she was three. Plus, my younger brother Cheng Xuan had been in Saarbrucken, Germany once, for a good thirteen years.

We did different things in Germany, mainly in the local universities, as a co-op study/research fellow, as a guest professor, as a guest engineer, as a kindergarten toddler, as a university preparation course in-taker, as a student, as a retiree, as a housewife and as a grandma in Germany, and we dealt with many people. None of them showed the characters of the Axes. What we learned from Germany was completely different. How do technical university staff run their university? Here I explain the German way of running one of their universities to my ex-schoolmates in China and the school's head/dean/ principal etc. nowadays. Other readers can skip this paragraph.

West Germany, the West Bank of the North Rhein, Aachen Technical University has more than 300 research institutes, each with only one director, who is also the only professor of the institute. He and each professor from these 300 institutes have a "one person, one vote" congress. There is also just one vote shared by tens of thousands of students, including graduate students. Other faculty members do not have the right to vote. This congress ruled the university. From the professors' votes (300) vs. all the votes (300/301: 99.7 percent), one can see this is absolutely a school where the professors hold power. The dean is the speaker of the professor's congress, and he has only one vote, not two. In 2003, I accompanied a delegation group sent by Tsinghua University China to universities in West Germany's (the two Germanys have been united for many years, and so should be called simply Germany) Heidelberg University expedition. On the university's philosopher's trail, I convinced their accompanying professor about the governing way of the above-mentioned Aachen University. You see, a Chinese professor is only a companion to his delegation group. The group's funder was the head. She was a woman from Tsinghua Zi Guang Company. The professor said, "I understand it. Please convince our great leader." Then I repeated it again to the head of the delegation. The head of the regiment didn't listen. It's OK with me. After more than ten years, Tsinghua is still like that, proudly ranked number one in China. The party secretary rules the school, the same as any other university in China. Axes cover China, including world-class universities. Internationally speaking, Tsinghua is declining in the world's university rankings.

7

University Relocation

Let's come back and continue my story about the Steel Courtyard. The Steel Courtyard had a major historic opportunity under the dictatorship of the Axes. It elevated the Steel Courtyard to the top third position of nearly 100 universities in Beijing at that time. Peking University, Tsinghua—they were always the top two. Now the Steel Courtyard becomes number three.

In 1969, it had been more than two years since Mao tricked students who had fought for him to go to the countryside. "The vast world, there is a great deal to do … It is necessary for the young intellectuals to go to the countryside and receive the re-education of the poor and lower peasants." In mid-1969, Mao moved his colleges and universities from Beijing to the countryside, and they all went to Province Jiangxi's—one of the poorest places in

China—Peking University and Tsinghua University. The Steel Courtyard also planned to go to Province Jiangxi and follow the top two. Even my father was sent to be the first pioneer team player. A ticket was on the dining table in my home.

Usually to get such a travelling ticket you must spend a night or two in long lines at the Beijing Railway Station ticket hall. Now it was free. It was not a good sign. Good things never come for free. The next day my father was to take the train to cross two thousand kilometres to stay and work there for a long time, maybe the rest of his life. He did not say goodbye to us, because it was the chance for him to serve his exile time. At that time, my brother had just been born, and was less than half a year old. Then there was a miracle. In the middle of that very night, the door was knocked on quickly and in a delightful way, like a heartbeat. My father's colleague had come and reported the good news that Chairman Mao, the Great Leader, had listened to his spy, the commissioner of the Beijing Municipal Revolutionary Committee, which seized the right of the former municipal government not to listen to Chairman Mao, Xie FuZhi, that North China still needed a steel academy. Mao meant that the Steel Courtyard should stay in Beijing and not relocate. His words were prioritized, of course. Other people had no right to talk and express their opinions at all. This latest supreme instruction had no written version on the record. Strange. In fact, in China, having no written record of such an important decision that impacts thousands of lives is quite common. Where had the Chinese Communist party hidden their registries? Nowhere. Where is the written order to open fire on the Tiananmen Square in Beijing in June 1989? Nowhere to be found.

Mu Jun, who was also the son of a dean at the Steel Courtyard, had a version of Zhou Enlai as follows: March 2nd, 1969, two armies fought on the treasure island on the Ussuri River on the China–Soviet Union border area. First, this border conflict confirmed that Soviet Union revisionist imperialism always wants to destroy China completely; second, there was a T-62 tank salvaged from the frozen river water, and its armoured parts were disassembled and taken to the metal-materials research desk of the Steel Courtyard in Beijing. How was the armoured steel made? Rockets, anti-tank weapons could not crack it. At most, they could make a mark on the armoured steel, just like a teacher's chalk hitting the blackboard: a point, and a point only.

Professor Mu Cheng Zhang, the father of my classmate from elementary school to university, Mu Jun, presided over this semi-military research project. He did not go home in the middle of the night. Premier Zhou En Lai came to visit the research group and called Professor Mu to report to him. Professor Mu asked the prime minister to give him several more days to figure out what on earth the revisionists put in the steel and alloy armoured plate. Then Chinese Central Government Premier Zhou Enlai went to report to Chairman Mao of the Chinese Communist party Central Military Committee ... the Axe's absolute head, eh? They agreed our Steel Courtyard should stay in Beijing and not move with the other institutions. The Steel Courtyard was lucky to stay in the capital, Beijing, becoming the first one in the country's metallurgical colleges and universities. In fact, the academic research level of the Beijing Steel Institute was not as good as the Northeast Institute of Technology in Shenyang, and the south is not as good as the Zhong Nan Mining and Metallurgy Institute in Chang Sha. Just because there was no relocation in this peacetime, preparing for war still requires steel and does not completely interrupt technical research and development (academic? There has never been an academic), so that the school site and the standard are not in place, the Steel Courtyard and other institutions tossed the relocation caused by the interruption of teaching research.

8

Family economy

What was family economic life before and after the Cultural Revolution? There were no banks. Wages were paid within institutions once a month in cash. The place where parents worked was usually called a unit, or "Dan Wei" in Chinese. Unit payday was the day when the finance section prepared a drawer of money, and each employee had an employee number. The number and the salary were handwritten on a paper roll. In one line, on one slip that belongs to you, it is written how much you earned that month, how much rent you pay, how much in water and electricity bills you pay, how much in co-op medical care you pay, how much union fees you pay, etc. You can see how much one can bring home, yours and others. There was no privacy. The money was wrapped in this slip. Each of the salaried people get it once a month. The difference was 18 yuan and 240 yuan (6-48 Canadian dollars a month). There was no float/promotion in ten years during the Cultural Revolution from 1966 to 1976. 18 yuan was the minimum living expense in that time. To keep your head above water, one needed these 18 yuan.

My uncle, Mr. Zhang Shan Xian, was paid 18 yuan a month to keep him alive at the beginning of the Cultural Revolution. His original salary of 240 yuan a month was suspended and on hold for an illegal investigation. It was concluded in my uncle's favour. Thank God. He was an underground supporter of the Chinese New Fourth Army and donated medical supplies in Shanghai during the time the Japanese troops conquered it along with a large part of China in World War II. He was captured by the Japanese gendarmerie and was tortured until he permanently lost his fertility, but he did not betray the Chinese military and civilian anti-Japanese underground activists. He was not only a good man, but also a hero. He was freed in the mid-cultural revolution. Immediately he benefitted from implementing the policy and paid the full 240 yuan a month. His previously suspended salaries were all paid to him. He got his job again, as the chief engineer of the Beijing Chemical Plant.

This Beijing Chemical Plant was established in Shanghai by my uncle, Mr. Zhang Shan Xian. In the 1950s there was a merger in national enterprises. All private sectors were merged into national ones against the private sector owners' wishes. In exchange, the private sector owners got salary payments for the rest of their careers. When my uncle's plant relocated to Beijing, he came to Beijing also. Believe or not, there was no chemical industry in Beijing in the 1950s. My uncle spent seven thousand yuan to get a quality house in downtown Beijing. It was located on Northeast 4th Avenue and furnished. The original owner was an Indonesian Chinese and returned to Beijing in 1949 or 1950. In the Cultural Revolution they suffered from every kind of suspicion: investigations, torture, illegal imprisonment, etc. The Cultural Revolution was not yet over, and he took the chance to go overseas. With another word, he ran away from China. He sold his house in Beijing to my uncle.

Now, with these seven thousand Yuan, it is impossible to buy the same house in the same location. I'm afraid one can't buy even half a square metre today. Some readers may question this: the sale/purchase of houses during the Cultural Revolution? How could it be? I tell you and all my readers: it's true. The seller was a famous overseas Chinese. He returned to China from overseas, then back overseas from China, thanks to his reputation. Thousands of ordinary overseas Chinese returned to mainland China in the 1950s and never got such chances to be abroad again. The house buyer was a pure nationalist, a chemical expert, an ex-capitalist, and a hero in World War II. Alone in his chemical expertise, Shanghai was the number-one chemical industry center in China. My uncle was the number-one chemist in Shanghai. The supplemental policy was opened to him for a little while on one side, and he could buy a house. This is an extreme example.

More commonly, how do people with merely dozens of dollars in wages support their families? Here's a look at the family economy. Salaries are not enough to support a family. A second economic source becomes a heavy priority. This is called "union subsidies." Every member of the salaried workforce is a union member. In a family, the union worker is the only person to earn wages, and seven or eight people are dependant on him. Then he is absolutely the subsidies earner, because his salary is all spent to buy food. And it can hardly cover the food cost. I'll make it clear to you. One-half kilogram of flour is 0.185 yuan, and 20 percent of the whole family's quantitative allotment could be flour, or "fine crops." You could buy a kind of white flour, which costs you more than 0.21Yuan/half kilogram. Various tickets in the rationing system are: flour tickets, rice tickets, crop tickets, peanuts oil tickets, and a purchase booklet, one page per month/family, with the possibility of buying a limited amount of side food (protein), such as 20 eggs per household per month, 1 kilo of pork meat per person per month, 2 kilos hallah meat, etc. Hallah meat is not sold to Sino Chinese at all, only to Muslims. Chicken? Duck? Fish? Seafood? They can be bought deep-frozen around Chinese New Year. In 1980, before the Spring Festival, Luna Festival, or Chinese New Year celebrations, my schoolmate Ms. Luo Ji was several hours in a long line outdoors to get some frozen fish for her family. Apparently, she saw my mom, her chemistry professor, who was also in the line but far behind her. She kindly invited my mom to join her in line. This saved my mom's daughter-in-law searching time (a Chinese mother has an obligation to find a wife for her son) and shortened my mom's outdoor waiting list in the cold winter. She became my wife in 1987. We both love my mom.

Continue our rationing supply. A quarter kilo of sugar per person per month; 100 grams sesame sauce, only in the Chinese New Years month; a quarter kilo of peanut oil a month; tofu per household per month 1 kilo, etc. Every year for clothing fabric we had 14 feet per person, cotton at 1.5 kilos. It's lucky to buy these things to our upper limit. Often a month would pass and side food was unavailable in small shops and large stores, like the co-op store chain. These quantitative supplies expired. The window of my kitchen faced the co-op store in the Steel Courtyard—as soon as something happened, some unknown food was delivered, I always jumped out of the kitchen window and ran into the store to line up first. Minutes later, my elder sister would walk into the store in the proper way, with a purchase booklet and money. What teamwork it took to fight hungry! I did this together with my elder sister from the ages of nine to fifteen. It was a kind of track-and-field basic training, my "housework." I was good at high jump, long jump, sprint, etc. thanks to this rush to get food rations.

I will come back to tell a story about the grain shop. In Southern China it is called a rice shop. People with a city or township registry have a rationing system supply, from birth to death, and every month more than a dozen pounds goes to the highest 35 pounds. In a six-person family, it costs 40 yuan to buy flour every month. Poor-quality rice is 0.152 yuan/lb. Good-quality rice is 0.213 yuan/lb. To buy rice, this family also must spend 30 yuan. To buy corn, 0.112 yuan/lb, they would have 15 yuan to spend. Right? This food expenditure is 85 yuan. With no meat or little protein, everyone eats more grains. In a family with more boys, they need more food. They try to get more food-ration tickets. I was a child labourer from the age of seven, a primary school first-grader to the age of fifteen and a middle schooler. The schools were the "employer" but didn't pay us for child labour, instead they paid us with the food ration tickets, one quarter kilo a day in paper, not in the form of food.

We did physical labour jobs year after year. Every year my classmates were forced to do a labour job for one day, one week or even one month, light and heavy duty. Whatever assign to us, we had to do it: agricultural work, the army soldier parade training, factory plant jobs. Girl students did not need this much food. They had to do the same jobs as male students. For girls it was not simply for food, it was hooked up to political preference. One could not simply state: "I do not want to become part of the labour class. I want to be myself." That is individualism, and it must be destroyed. Fourteen- and fifteen-year-old girls had to bend over and plant young rice seedlings into muddy fields or remove weeds by hand all day long. This was not good on their still-growing backs. School staff forced them to do this labour, which was not only hard, but also body-damaging. It was the vice principal of my school, Mr. Xie Guo Dong, and not the teachers who made this brutal decision. My poor female schoolmates stood barefoot in the mud. When they could not suffer any longer standing on their bare feet, they had to stand on their knees in the mud. Grasshoppers, otters or whatever else was in the mud would climb on their/our thin legs, sucking their/our flesh and not much blood. Forgive me here! I really can't write any more in detail. It was painful. We were suffering. We should not have gotten this kind of punishment in name of "practice" or "exercise." 40% of my schoolmates got dysentery in the labourer camp and we had to withdraw from the dirty site. We were defined as the successors of communism, but in real life we were deeply damaged, in body and mind. If communism has a bright future where people live a good life and are happy, why should we live such a miserable life now? We should learn how to share equal rights, and to live a high standard of life with each other. At least it beats capitalism. We dare not speak about our doubts, then and now.

As mentioned earlier, a family of six spends 85 yuan a month on grain food. It is surely not enough to eat. What is the salary level of 85 yuan (10–12 US dollars)? My father was a university lecturer at that time, the highest grade in the middle class. He was paid only 89.5 yuan a month. It was impossible for him to raise a family of six. Thanks go to my mother, who was able to make 78 yuan a month at that time. My mom was a junior lecturer at that time before and during the Cultural Revolution. In short, other people who couldn't support their families had to go to the union to apply for subsidies. The maximum subsidy per union member per month was 30 yuan, the bottom line was zero or negative—everybody pays the union membership fees. The union membership fee was about 0.13 yuan/month. Do you dare to not listen? Do you dare say socialism is no good? Do you say communism is a lie?

Do you dare say Chairman Mao is not the great savior of the people? Say anything against the communists and you can't get a subsidy, and the elimination of the subsidy would have killed this family. The political tendency to be loyal to the Communist party is, in the final analysis, the sustaining economic problem there, the family economy. Loyalists in China are mostly poor men. You have a slight doubt, are unfaithful to the Communist party, don't show that you love the Communist party, then wait a moment! You will starve! You will freeze! Because the rationing system was so tightly controlled, if you did not get stuff there, you would get anything elsewhere.

Nylon or plastic stuff was not so common at that time. Cotton was the only clothing material that could keep one from being cold. Underwear? I'd never heard of it. Wearing a vest without sleeves was not allowed at school, so simply do not wear a vest. A Zhong Shan dress or Mao suit was worn without underwear nor skirt. Tallman has a common nickname: waste of fabric, waste of food. The homemade cotton blanket for the average person was not long enough to cover their bodies from below the neck to the toes. In the 1976-77 winter, the Steel Courtyard stopped supplying heat to all its residents' homes. In the winter nights, the room temperature dropped down to 6–7° Celsius in a north-facing room. I had to sleep there. The other four members of my family crowded in the south-facing room to sleep. At the next morning's wake-up time, it was up to my sister to visit me in the north-facing room. She was happy when she saw me still alive, breathing. Getting out of the bed could be a challenge. I was wearing an exported "Aid to Africa" pullover, a very good quality navy-blue round-collar long-sleeved velvet. Velvet clothes for Africans' kids were too much. People there did not buy them. Then they were transferred to domestic sales, 6 yuan a piece, eh? I wore it for three seasons, year after year, and I grew up in it. My arms got longer and longer, and the velvet seemed to shrink until one day I could not wear it as my school uniform any longer, so I turned it into my underwear. Its long sleeves became short ones. It still looked like new. There was not a single opening nor loosely sewn lines. There was no fading either. For what reason did Chinese Communists support such a massive amount of stuff to the world revolution? The best quality of everything was exported, and the same stuff—if they could not pass the quality control or had some other issue—would stay in

China and be sold to the poor and low-class peasants like me, among others.

Let me get out of my bed first, before I die from freezing. Goosebumps rise on my body almost every day. It's not a disease. It's being poor. Under the tight control of this hungry and cold life in the rationing system, what else is the so-called "class struggle"? And what is the socialist practice, the communist ideal/dream? It's all deceitful. It is subsidizing slavery. If you don't listen to the master, you will have nothing to eat and nothing to wear; you don't have a resource to fill out your hungry tummy. You listen to your master, and there is only one kind of material for everyone. Your food and clothing, your income, is only enough to sustain you half nightly; you must keep wanting, you must always be obedient, and show your loyalty to the Communist party.

I had a neighbor, little Li. He was the editor/typographer of the Steel Courtyard's printing workshop. His name was Li You Ren. The Steel Courtyard had thousands of people in its population. Among them were many surnamed Li, but he exclusively ranks as number one "Little Li." This was called "Jiang Hu." Jiang Hu was an unofficial place where people from different classes got together and theoretically/practically exercised their Kung Fu, or any kind of martial arts, and they have an unofficial name or credentials. Jiang Hu exists but nobody can tell others what on earth it is. The best novel to tell the Jiang Hu story during the Song Dynasty is *By the Water*. Xiao Li or Little Li was typical of such people. He was the goalkeeper of the Steel Courtyard staff soccer team. His daily pants were significantly better than everyone else's pants. Maybe it's because he was tall and had long legs. His bicycle was also significantly better than the ordinary ones, made of a manganese steel alloy, with wire brakes, a fully wrapped chain case, and a rotary bell, black in colour. Of course, every single bicycle in that time was black. Now, you could call him the most handsome guy in the Steel Courtyard. He made himself famous in a celebration event. China got her seat at the United Nations in 1970. There was a party, and each branch had to have a program for theatre showtime. Little Li's printing workshop had a theatre piece to show, too. And his role was the American ambassador to the United Nations. On the stage, his makeup was funny: long nose, white suit, leather shoes. The Republic of China's (Taiwan) ambassador was chasing him to secure his job and to secure the original seat for Taiwan. He gave the Taiwanese the following words and made the audience happy.

"I hate you, hate you, hate you!"

"Your face is so long."

"Why did you follow me into the bathroom?"

"Be a man."

Ridiculously, in order to stigmatize the Americans, Little Li, my Uncle Li and my neighbour (I should call every male employee at the Steel Courtyard "uncle" and the female ones "auntie"), he painted a layer of blue and green on his own face. My first time meeting an actual American man was in 1985. (Earlier I did learn American English from female Americans. They were foreign language teachers to the Steel Courtyard funded by the United Nations Developing Org.) He was not very different from that stereotype, which Uncle Li had built up fifteen years prior, except for the color of his face. He was the director of energy, a professor at the University of Utah, John A. Herbst.

I will now come back and continue my story about the Uncle Li. He struggled so hard to get a son after he had two daughters. This was the biggest challenge of the Chinese nationwide one-child policy, or birth control. His challenge broke my family's economics in the Cultural Revolution. I don't mind, but I'd like to share his way of breaking through together with you, the readers of this book. My family and Uncle Li's shared an apartment, #5 resident building, unit 110. My family of six people lived in two bedrooms. Each room was 12 square metres, or 130 square feet. Uncle Li had a family of five people, occupying a large bedroom, 18 square metres or 194 square feet. There was no sitting room, two families shared one kitchen and a squat pit-type toilet with a flushing water tank without a washbasin, Soviet Union standard. Ha. It was too crowded for eleven people to live together in a three-bedroom apartment. We were as intimate as a family. Uncle Li took me swimming in the petroleum college outdoor swimming pool, where he taught me how to breathe in and out on the water surface. From then on, back at the tough swimming pool in the Steel Courtyard, we'd try to win a splashing-water fight, which is when two sides splash water against each other, and the rules say not to allow the body to have contact with each other. I really did not lose any such fight thanks my Uncle Li's instruction. A few summers passed, and Uncle Li's wife Auntie Li delivered two daughters, and became pregnant again with the third baby. This time it was a boy. But this undermines birth control in the Steel Courtyard. One violated the rules, regulations, policies, so now the whole Steel Courtyard was under review. Everybody's bonus was canceled. Uncle Li was suspended from his salary and the union's subsidy was suspended, too. The whole family had no livelihood, the family Li also had to support Uncle Li's mother-in-law's mother, an old woman from Province Shan Xi. She stayed at home, helped to do some housework, cared for her great-granddaughter. She had some time to show me how to cook pancakes. My skill of being a chef was built at my age of ten, eleven, or twelve.

I won't talk too much about food and cooking skills. Uncle Li's family was going to break down with no food to eat. The printing workshop he worked for did not pay his wages, the unions did not support with subsidies, and the members of the union stood up in time. They used their external power to sponsor Little Li. What's the external power? A movie. Play the moonlight movie and generate the box office revenues. The large institutes had an outdoor movie theater. Two utility poles held a white screen up in an open-air flat and wide area, and the audience could sit on both sides and enjoy a moonlight movie night for free or 0.05 yuan per person. The union people could borrow movie copies from the film distribution company for free. The movie theatre site at the Steel Courtyard was first located outside the Family Ding compound, the northwest corner of the large playground. Later, because its projector chamber was a small detached house far enough from other houses, it was converted into a liquefied petroleum gas can supply station (LPG distributer). And the movie theatre site was moved to the big dining hall in winter and its backyard outside in summer. The projector chamber had two directions to put movie images onto, inside of the big dining hall and outside of it. Wide-screen projectors were there. We were able to view wide-screen movies (24 mm film) for a quite reasonable ticket price, 0.10 yuan per person.

Long story short, the union members generated ticket office revenues and donated them all to the Little Li, my neighbour, Uncle Li. Unionists in China oversaw organizing events for everybody's spare-time activities only. They had no power at all to represent union members regarding tariff negotiations, employment, and so on. A positive image of a union leader in any Chinese institution is that he/she has all kinds of tickets.

Sports-event tickets, movie tickets, exhibition tickets, trade-show tickets, bicycle tickets, and finally, birth-control tickets, in his/her pocket. Basically, all these tickets were free. But for good reason, people never complained about the symbolic charges. The Communist party knew how to make people happy by organizing free, low-cost entertainment events. And the organizer was always the union leader. His assistants were union activists and they worked for free. Make sense? The audience pays 5 cents per person for a black-and-white movie night, 10 cents for colour movies, widescreen movies, foreign movies. Those foreign movies were excellently translated into Chinese Mandarin. Little Li was a union activist. On movie nights, he set up temporary entrances every few metres in rings surrounding the "movie theater" to collect ticket money on-site. One helps the others and builds up a kind of brotherhood. When he needed something, he would ask his brothers/colleagues instead of the Communist party. Union activists helped their brother Little Li after movie nights. They harvested coins and brought them all to Little Li, not even one coin was swallowed by any of his brothers. This was to show their solidarity against the birth-control policy. Little Li was acknowledged. He already knew in that time that the birth-control policy was not a lawful act. I respect him in this regard. Other people, including me, were confused. We didn't know who was more powerful, the Communist party or the law. Two thousand audience members could generate 100 yuan a movie night. 5 cents per person! All the residents in the Steel Courtyard showed their support for Little Li to rescue his broken family economy. We played the latest movies and replayed the most popular old movies almost once a week and made the Steel Courtyard change its nickname to the Sports and Film Academy. My Uncle Li, who was hit by the national policy of family planning, had an unexpected harvest from his brotherhood. And because of him we got a chance to watch all the films that could be released publicly at that time. Not even one was not played. Not even one of us kids were absent. Do you know what a running film is? It's just a few of the same movie copies that are shown at the same time. Of course, this is so-called because there are one or two rolls of a copy playing with a time difference. In this time difference, a motorcyclist was riding a motorbike like a crazy person, transporting copies back and forth between two moonlight movie sites. This is called a running film.

In the age of material poverty, a copy of a movie runs two or more scenes on the same night, entertaining the general public who suffered during the day. Every classic line, every character in our young hearts occupies an irreplaceable position, but we will also never forget the joy of the ode. To this day, when we get together, we keep repeating these things:

"A Li Xiang Yang, scared you into this?"

"Uncle Thomas was an officer, and he made me an officer."

"Zhang Jun Zhang, please look at the party's share, pull out your hands, bail me out of here."

"You're not real soldiers, you don't understand the tactics."

Go with it, and it's popular. The proudest is the revolutionary song revision singing, "Going to a shooting exercise" into the following music:

Qian Guan drives a horse cart, Sun Fu asks to do him a favor: sell his hazel nuts, peppers and mushrooms for extra money.

Qian Guang's wife is smart: "Why did you pay him two bucks more?"

Qian Guang says: "That is wool out of sheep."

Qian Guang's wife spits water on his face.

"Hey! Splash him with water!"

In the autumn and winter seasons, the first thin snow came in a hurry. Crops harvested in the fields were brought to large institutes such as the Steel Courtyard on a large scale. What was the point? Sweet potatoes, cabbage, leeks. Then there's coal. It was heavy, and the general carriage donkey-cart tricycle couldn't pull it. It would be delivered in the tow bucket of ten-wheeled Cara. Ten-wheeled trucks are the largest ones we had ever seen as children, in 1960–70. The eight-ton Yellow River domestic truck could not do this job. A four-ton domestic Liberty truck could not do this job. Only the huge Czech-made Tetra trailer could do this job. The Tetra drove into our yard, and its powerful engine noise brought everybody out into the Steel Courtyard. Numbers 1, 2, 3, and 4 resident buildings got the message first. They were close to the north entrance, where heavy-duty trucks came in and out delivering food, fuel, construction materials—everything but the milk truck. The milk truck delivered fresh milk daily and picked up empty milk bottles from the main entrance, the west entrance. There were queues of children in a line to the empty grounds on the west side of the co-op store yard. Sometimes we had to queue up all night. Multi-children families had advantages over single-child ones—kids would take turns in line, each standing for several hours. Cabbage was delivered in a human conveyor chain, one by one handing cabbages off the car and onto the ground. Sweet potatoes were carried off, stacked on the ground, and sold. A kilo of food stamps could buy 5 kilos of sweet potatoes.

In famine years, when there was not enough food, the relief came once a year, and was just sweet potatoes at harvest time. Poor families wanted to stock some 500 pounds or more, rich families wanted at least 100 pounds. The difference between rich and poor was five times then. Why is it so much wider today? Sweet potatoes don't freeze well and can't be placed in an air-tight container either. You need a cellar to stock them. They cannot simply be placed on the floor of the house, under the bed. So, in the Steel Courtyard, every lot or space between buildings was ideal to dig a vegetable cellar to store the sweet potatoes. Every family had to build one. We used to live a squirrel's life, eh? Huang Lu Jun, the most capable classmate of mine, could dig five vegetable cellars a day. He passed away before he reached fifty. They figured that he grew up physically overstretched and overworked, and the epidemic ended up earlier than usual. He not only dug his own family's vegetable cellar, but he also dug many others for his teachers, classmates, neighbours.

In the residential courtyard, between two trees, there was often a rope, a string for drying sweet potatoes. Playground games were cancelled for the season, mainly for this purpose. Private ownership was respected, even of the poorest-quality food in the dying famine. There was no jeopardizing our food. We needed it so badly that the cooked food was very often taken directly from pots before it was placed in bowls or dishes.

This scenario continued until1980s, when the Steel Courtyard canteen also built a large ground vegetable cellar near the public shower room, which contained a large amount of cabbages—truckloads, the whole ten-wheeled Tetra truckload of cabbages. The joy of finally having enough food ended in a less-decent orgy in 1981. The Chinese national women's volleyball team won the world championship. By then, the dormitories were equipped with black-and-white television sets called Hungary 19 inches. Students set up the TV for each faculty in front of the first-floor window with the screen facing out, so that all students in this dormitory, 500-plus people, could watch the live sports event, broadcasted by the only television channel, which was and is called CCTV: Chinese Central Television. Next to the student audience were these cabbages, just unloaded onto the ground, having not had time to be put into the cellar. Or they were cabbages from the vegetable cellar brought up to bask in the sun to reduce their external moisture. The winning moment was broadcast on the small television screen: the Chinese girls beat the Japanese ones in the 5th game 17-15, and the top girl Lang Ping was only twenty at the time. The Steel Courtyard canteen winter storage cabbages were all thrown into the sky.

Of course, it was the result of the excitement of college students. They turned a sport victory celebration into a cabbage fest. There was a cabbage shortage that winter, even though it was a cabbage bumper harvest the season before. The canteen offered its cheapest dish, boiled cabbage, at an increased price, from 0.10 yuan per portion to 0.15. And the price has never fallen back to 0.10 yuan again. Overjoyed students impressed the women's volleyball team. When they heard about this craziness, they sent the Beijing women's volleyball team to the Steel

Courtyard. The team was also the national champions, the best players were on the national team. Every girl player was warmly greeted as a national hero there in the Steel Courtyard. The show was on. The university student men's volleyball team challenged the national hero girls for only ten points in one game. The girls had more strategic play than the men had. They went through ten different tactics. Spike, back slip, short-flat-fast, plus three, front fly, back fly, back-row jump attack, blocking, setter's trick, etc. The boys' Steel Team could only spike from the #4 position in the volleyball court. Also, because they did not have enough food, and their meal quality was not up to the provincial sports teams' standard—say, 97 yuan/month, "eat as much as you like," although our school sports team meal was 0.40 yuan a meal per day. It was the most expensive dish at that time. The poor go to study. The rich play sports. That is common.

There was not enough food and people were hungry and being hungry in winter makes one feels colder. Every winter from November 15 to March 15, all buildings were heated by the boiler room of the Steel Courtyard, from what was called the central heating system. The heating medium was water. And the fuel to heat up the water was coal. We had two boiler rooms to pump out hot water in the winter season, among other two hot drinking-water boiler rooms in the Steel Courtyard. The boilers in the Steel Courtyard needed about a thousand tons of anthracite coal every year.

Coal was also shipped by a big truck with a huge trailer, Tetra was again hired, and it was transported for several days to pile up a coal mountain. The boiler room recruited operators from outside. They worked and burned coal for generating hot water 24/7. For two years during the Cultural Revolution, my father was forced to work as a boiler operator in there. As a university lecturer he could not deliver his lectures at the podium. His salary was still paid the same—89.50 yuan a month. They were good at turning a useless man into a useful man.

Of course, there were no students to attend universities in the first five years of the Cultural Revolution. Then my father was sent to the boiler room to burn the coal. The boiler was a manually operated industrial boiler. That is to say, the job of operating it is an extremely tough job, from manually transporting the coal to feeding the boiler to pulling out slag, adding in cold water, pumping out hot water, and so on. Count the amount of physical-labour jobs he did: hundreds of tons of coal was to be shovelled from the coal pile uphill into a trolley, then the trolley was pushed into the boiler room to the side of the boiler, shovelled in, and then 10–20 percent of the ash of fuel coal is picked out of the boiler, loaded onto a trolley, and taken to the slag heap to be dumped. Every day, the manual loading and unloading capacity of a boiler worker is tens of tons in weight. This is not an exaggeration. The shift was twelve hours on duty, then rest twenty-four hours off duty. Every day he had to pour the slag, and he got the external strengthening of physical labor, but the environment was dirty, dusty, high risk, and almost every year there was a boiler explosion. Migrant workers got killed and injured in the Steel Courtyard boiler room, and the entire courtyard had no job more inferior than this work.

I doubted that the kitchen knives/Axes were going to use a boiler explosion to kill my father. But my father was invincible. Two winters passed. He not only survived, but also rebuilt his body and soul. He could fall asleep no matter when and where. And he never overslept. What a skill that was! He completely bid farewell to depression, nervous breakdowns, sleep disorders, illness, whatever. He became a member of the "working class" physically and mentally according to himself, but not recognized by Axes. As to why none of the intellectuals who worked in the boiler room of the Steel Courtyard were not killed or injured in any accidents, this was thanks to the brains they had, armed with scientific and technological knowledge. In my father's case, he was an expert in physical chemistry, specializing in dealing with heat, temperature, and pressure through the three laws of thermodynamics, from theories to practice, operating a stove/boiler, etc., including water/steam boilers. These were really his strengths. Migrant workers did not have this kind of knowledge. They often operated the boiler incorrectly, which led to fatal accidents. A round check before any on/off switching is the key.

I'll come back and tell stories about keeping warm in winters. The heating of the residence near the boiler room was relatively good, while the heating of the residence far away from the boiler room was poor. The heatsink/ radiator did not reach room temperature. Of course, it was lower than everyone's body temperature. It would take someone's body heat away from his/her body. How did the residents there survive the winter? Solar. Don't laugh.

Solar is the premier energy source. So how does solar energy get into the bedroom? It is our cotton blanket on the sunny day. We would hang it outdoors to get sunshine on it to gain solar energy. In the afternoon when the temperature reached the highest of the day, we would take the blanket full of solar energy home. At night this cotton quilt was warm and soft, and exuded a kind of human sweat, urine, and sunshine violet odour. You experience it and you'll love it. I'm not a pervert.

During the Cultural Revolution there were about three construction heat. The first heat was the construction of bomb shelters. The threat of nuclear-bomb airstrikes was within range, and the China–Mongolia border was just 300 kilometres from the nearest location: the Chinese capital, Beijing. The Soviet revisionists (we used to call Russians this) sent 1 million troops into Mongolia, armed with tanks. This was verified by me when I passed by on an international express train in the capital of Mongolia, Ulan Bator, on June 1, 1989. Many Soviet Union Red Army soldiers and military officers, some of them with handheld coded briefcases, entered and exited their exclusive platform in the railway station. In the late 1960s and early 1970s, the Red Army of the Soviet Union was about to launch rockets carrying nuclear warheads to strike China. The first goal was Beijing. The action was called "the surgery." And it was legendarily stopped by our American friends. The Red Amy tanks could enter China and drive to Beijing in only one day, so everyone was rushing to build bomb shelters, hiding cellars. It was said that during air raids shattered glass can hurt people, so paste paper was stuck on home windows to reduce the glass in the air so it wouldn't hurt people. The trick probably came from World War II, when Japan bombarded China and Germany hit London with air strikes, where the local people were so hostile. People had to hide during the air raids, and the bomb shelters were far away. The Steel Courtyard south of its resident buildings, numbers 1, 2, 3, and 4, and at the northwest corner of the big track and field (with a double 400 metre track) playground, the tennis yard today, was surrounded by barbed wire, where it was filled with building materials in the time of the Cultural Revolution. An old cadre surnamed Ding oversaw building shelters within the Steel Courtyard. Therefore, the in-stock construction-material place was called Ding's Villa. Mr. Ai Ya Wen, the principal of the elementary school attached to the

Steel Courtyard, was dismissed from his position and was holed up in Ding's Villa in the Cultural Revolution. He became the only man at Ding's Villa. When the Soviet Union was about to start a war, the threat was so serious that all the Steel Courtyard residents were digging bomb shelters, blanking, brickmaking, firing kilns, and building reinforced concrete bow prefabs, and when the Soviet Union revisionists were not pushing, the threat was eased and the Steel Courtyard people took a break. Only one person continued to build bomb shelters— punching, digging drainage, sieving sand. This person was the principal Ai Ya Wen. He was wearing the hat of a historical counter-revolutionist and doing heavy-duty/ dangerous labour under the supervision of other people as a corrective course/term. Anyone can be that supervisor, and a few people pranked/humiliated him.

I was a seven- or eight-year-old little boy. I went to a pile of dirt and viewed the deep hole, which was for the not-yet-built bomb shelter. He was at the bottom of the deep hole. I thought that if I fell into it, I could never climb out. He kept his dignity. His clothes were always in a clean and neat condition, although the shoulders were faded. He never wore a straw hat. That is the icon of a peasant. He would never become one. His revolt was silent but firm. He never showed his guilty face. His back was always straight. When he walked, his hands were never found in his pocket or sleeves, unlike others. Their backs were bent. Their guilty faces accompanied them their whole lives, even when they held the power. Principal Ai was one of the most well-educated and polite people I had ever seen in my youth. I respected him very much, but he confused me. Whenever I went to watch him work on the bomb-shelter construction site he thought that I was supervising him, reporting anything negative. This was a misunderstanding. Very often he was left alone without supervision. That was the labour camp, too. He was a public enemy and under everybody's supervision. "A public enemy can be drowned in the ocean of people's war." Mao said so. I couldn't see my dad, so I visited Principal Ai instead.

My father was supervised in the labour camp in the Steel Courtyard and everywhere else. Red Axes over China—my book's title means this. He was carrying bricks from a dry, hot brick kiln, along with many other suppressed labourers. The brick kiln was in the southwest corner of the metal physics building, which is now the site of the corrosion building or the metallography building. The four fellows of the Chinese Academy of Sciences, Wei Shou Kun (1908–2014), Xiao Ji Mei (1915–2014), Ke Jun (1919–2018), and one more whose name I cannot recall were the only four academic fellows who worked in the Steel Courtyard. They were the highest-ranked scientists in China. They were also forced to work as janitors in the early days of the Cultural Revolution, and their common place of sanitation was eight washrooms in four stock buildings, the metallography building, where they performed their high-end research in their special field; say, stainless-steel metallurgy, metallography, and so on. These kinds of academic work were put aside for daily sanitation. These eight toilets immediately became the favourite place to go for everyone in the Steel Courtyard. Look at our top scientists, they brought the cleanliness of the toilets to the next level. They used to live and study in Germany, Great Britain and the U.S. You want to learn anything from European and Americans? Let's start by cleaning up your place first. The attitude of academics to sweeping the toilet floor is an extension of the spirit of scientific exploration. Through practice and theory the mop was washed, but not used to wipe the floor on the same day. Only when the mop had been made soft with some moisture, not water droplets, was it used to wipe the floor, and the floor was cleaned and polished, without any flakes. Have a look at these two Chinese characters "干净" Our academics understand it in the right way, how the Chinese character-inventor Cang Jie original designed it for no misunderstanding: cleanliness means dry—less water. Right? Academics who cleaned toilets were absolutely the cleanest ones; it was no wonder people went to worship the toilets the top scientists sanitized.

The second heat of construction in the Cultural Revolution was slightly smaller in scale. We were tired of running national and international projects. They did not bring us any benefits. Besides, the whole of China spent some ten years building a bridge across the Yang Ze River in Nanking, which today is broken, not in use and phasing on demolition, and the ocean cargo ship Dong Feng, which could carry ten thousand tons of coal and rice, and could not go into the deep blue ocean but could transport goods along the Chinese coast instead. I was on her board in 1976. Shameful errors could be found everywhere. These were covered up. And these two projects were the "greatest victories of Mao Ze Dong," the "greatest victories of the

Cultural Revolution." All our construction materials were put into bomb shelters, with nothing left over for residence buildings. The underground work/bunkers/bomb shelters leaked, and water filled them all. The Chinese population was growing but people had nowhere to live. Every room was turned into a bedroom then. Kitchens had to be moved to the hallway, stairwell, outdoors, kitchenette, tree house, small garden, a chicken nest, etc. An apartment on the ground floor has advantages. It can automatically expand its living area. A small piece of land in front of the window is surrounded, and inside there is everything one could imagine: stove, flowerpot, chicken cage, can, rope, bicycle, aqua pond, new and used building materials, and so on. The rented interior furniture was also slowly substituted with a homemade sofa, a pair of single sofas, and a coffee table. My cousin Sa Ben Ren also made a Simmons bed for his mother, my auntie #1, Cheng Shu Shun. This masterpiece was made with wire-cord strap, wire reed: an authentic Simmons single bed. This was the most modern bed in our house. I also learned the Western furniture production process and production standards from watching my handy cousin's housework. After all, the financial resources were limited, and the furniture production time is a little too long. My cousin made 18 yuan a month in apprentice wages, but a reed was 4–5 yuan each, a single bed mattress needs forty to fifty reeds. Wood frames, fabrics, tools, etc. were not counted, but they were also more than 200 yuan.

The third construction heat was after the Tang Shan earthquake in 1976, when several earthquake-resistant sheds suddenly appeared in the Steel Courtyard and in northern China, none of which were heavy and none of which were built according to drawings/blueprints. There was a demand for houses, buildings. People smartly took the excuse of this earthquake to better their living conditions, enlarge their living spaces. You can imagine how happy people were when they could live in houses built by themselves. Is it the nature of human beings? Or do other species have this common sense? Birds live in the nests they build. Bunnies live in the holes they dig. Beavers live in their excellently built lodges with the entrance under the water to keep residents safe. And they are so friendly, they allow other animals to share the lodge and they even share food with them for free. They were all redneck pieces.

Ideas popped up for brainstorming for a while. Action follows an idea, or just a feeling of one's own, a smart one or a stupid one, it doesn't matter. Keep busy, keep doing something to use this chance. We were not allowed to realize our own ideas for decades. We enjoyed this creative work, a good feeling of being liberated, of being yourself. The miracle is that none of these ugly-looking houses collapsed, completely resisting the aftershocks that followed the strong strikes of our Mother Earth. I built one for my family of five. A beam is a long thick wooden board, wired/roped onto two cement poles, which are used to set up barbed wire. I have mentioned the barbed wire several times. It is so common in China. Maybe the barbed wire production in China is "proudly" the world's number one. Such a structure is called a "lamp on monkey's head" in the redneck class. The monkey is flexible and not tough. When the stress comes it will run away. "Lamp on the monkey's head" means it is unreliable and not strong. Even so, my DIY house did not collapse until the Steel Courtyard demolished it together with others one night in 1978.

At the beginning of the 1980s, the Chinese Communist Leader Dong Xiao Ping cut his army by 1 million soldiers. All the veterans from the engineering troop became construction workers and they founded six infrastructure group companies in Beijing. Dong avoided mutiny in this way—smart, eh? He got enough support from the army to get power, and the army secured his political power by escorting him right into Beijing, even without weapons. These construction workers were all his guards, like they were before. Citizens in Beijing and political enemies of Dong Xiao Ping did not realize it until he passed away in 1997. They were all happy that their great leader was building houses for them in the name of bettering intellectuals' lives first, retiring them all in Beijing (the greatest honour when they retire). He was greater than Mao. Oh my God. Mao was God to the Chinese people until then.

Back to my DIY house. The "bed" in the earthquake-resistant shed was the square cement pipe of the heating unit just underground in the Steel Courtyard—warm in winter and cool in summer. The ground is earth, but the wall cannot be only soil. When the loess and lime mix into a solid, it is called "hammered clay." Mongolians prepare their beef this way. A Mongolian soldier could carry a whole ration of beef on horseback. The beef is dewatered by hammering it in the extremely cold weather and, more importantly, the full protein free of water is ultra-light. We Sino build our houses with non-structural walls in this way, too, to attempt to remove water from clay.

Lime story: For a better-quality wall for my DIY house, I went to get a two-wheeled trolley/barrel. In the middle of the night, three of us sneaked into the elementary school attached to the Steel Courtyard. There was a ton of lime inventory. We shovelled it all into our barrel. The poor-quality barrel was leaking. It spilled lime along our track home. The white powder lime marked the way, like track and field playground lines. Mr. Ban, who was the only caretaker at our elementary school, lived in the school preparation room. He woke up in the middle of the night. He followed us several times, collecting the evidence he needed. We didn't even qualify as long fingers. Shame.

The next day we three were on the information board located at the major intersection of the Steel Courtyard. Citation! We were teenagers. We didn't mean to do anything against the revolution. Soon after this, people forgave and forgot us. The intersection was a big political centre for all students, university staffs and residents. In the Cultural Revolution, "DaZiBao" was there on the temporally wall, where it was specially built for this kind of propaganda. The so-called "DaZiBao" zone, or big-font paperwork area, was so popular that they were everywhere in China. They so badly damaged the positive images of great leaders, experts, officers, among others, by telling people at large about their leaders' background, privacy, crimes, suspicious activity, etc. There were so many who wanted to write, and so many curious people who wanted to read about other people's dark sides and not-so-glorious pasts. That wall was cheap, sorghum skin and other crops made up its mats, and it was nailed to a wooden pile of framework. Its top was also built of rainproof eaves. All walls were lit by lamps. It offered convenience to those people or Axes to be able to do their crimes in the darkness, which was to put their paperwork onto the wall nightly. The Axes/authors never signed their real names to it. Too bad. They knew it was a crime to slander others. These wall-building materials were ideal for a DIY house, but all our naughty children and others were afraid to get those things. They were politically relevant notices, so once caught, we would be persecuted as participating in the "destruction of the Cultural Revolution," the "destruction of the great leader Chairman Mao's great strategic deployment," and being a "current counter-revolutionist." These charges would not only destroy yourself but hurt your family as well. In fact, the small warehouse attached to the elementary school was in a fertilizer station in the northeast corner of its playground. Strictly speaking, the lime there was prepared for hardening the ground or alkalinized/neutralized fertilizer. On this piece of land was poured human stool and urine, all from the septic tanks in surrounding universities and other courtyards. It was the real organic fertilizer that was transported there by donkey-drawn carriage. These stinky things were dried with solar energy, creating a piece of cracked manure. Alas! The primary school we went to was smelly. It's all true. Vegetables at that time could never be eaten raw/fresh/uncooked. The reason is that they were contaminated through this kind of human manure fertilizer. The leaves had all kinds of virus, bacteria, and dirt, etc. Eating them would result in hepatitis, running tummy being the lightest symptom. Wash them before eating? Nice try. The tap water might be contaminated in China, too. It is better to eat bullshit directly, rather than human! Forgive me. Bulls and cows are vegetarians at least.

When I went to the Western world in June 1989, I cooked and fried vegetables at home almost every day. The vegetables, whether they were ground-growing leaves or underground clumps, picked from the vine, or grown through soilless cultivation, I would never wash them a second time. Cold dishes and hot ones, fresh cut, fresh cooked directly, but I haven't suffered any disease caused by contamination ever since. This huge difference—can you tell? Why Chinese people must drink boiled water, and the people in the Western world don't? Whether it is bottled water or tap water, all ready to drink. The source has a problem.

Write something light.

During the Cultural Revolution, as a little boy yet to grow up on an urban university campus, I had to do the housework: carrying coal from the apartment building's front door into our own kitchen; digging vegetable cellars; pouring cabbage; picking up milk bottles while returning empty ones; buying steamed bread, rice, flour, sweet potatoes; bringing them home in big sacks; processing vegetables and chopping melons; cutting rice cakes; cutting bamboo shoots; and so on.

Let's start with moving coal briquettes. There was a coal preparation/briquette plant in the northwest corner of the Steel Courtyard which produced briquettes and honeycomb coal made from anthracite (smokeless coal) powder, and soil and a little lime with water. Honeycomb coal was pressed, while the briquettes were rolled by a double-axle roller machine. Going to this plant to watch the machine operation was also fun. Later I became an engineer. These two machines in the coal preparation plant in the Steel Courtyard played a key role in my decision-making process. They inspired me a lot.

When I worked at the Premier Candle Inc. in Mississauga, Ontario, Canada from 1997–1998, I could run its candle forming/casting machine without training. It pressed wax powder into a pillar candle. It was just like the briquette machine I saw in the briquette plant.

Anyway, I am interested more in industrial electrical-mechanical-related things than I am in the metallurgical/chemical/environmental engineering stuff. The production of briquettes is good; the finished goods were brought by the mechanical conveyor belt to a warehouse, which is fully automated. And the products of honeycomb coal would be removed by the plant workers, half men and half women. They were then moved to the trolley by hand, and manually pushed to the drying field, and the wind passing by would remove the water contained therein, so that the honeycomb coal became dry and hard. We didn't call it honeycomb coal, we called it "coal cake" instead. Then they were removed again by hand to a three-wheeled flatbed cart, which was pulled by a female worker. She could not simply ride and paddle the cart. Her muscles could not bear the weight of the fully loaded cart. Each cart carried hundreds of coal cakes, large and small, and a few pieces of ignition cake, which is fine coal powder mixed with wood chips/sawdust and other flammable fuels, even gun-firing powder in black, used for igniting fire on the coal cake piled on top of it. A few hundred pieces of coal cake were manually moved by the poor female worker and taken to the front door of the residence building. She manually unloaded them all to the ground, one batch after another—different orders for various apartment/families—then collected money and drove her empty tricycle cart away, back to the coal preparation plant. She had to go back and forth several times a day. Her career life was extremely hard.

After that, moving the honeycomb coal/cake from the building's front door to my kitchen was my housework. I had to find the right pile of honeycomb coal on a piece of coal cake, on which was written my house number in white chalk. My life had such a specific meaning: it was my responsibility for moving them home without damages, from the first to the last piece. Poems and travel far away from home (fantasy) were not available at that time. Plastic film records of revolutionary pop songs and music on its recorder also had to be forgotten. English-language tuition records, "Linguaphon," were put into paper bags. I had to move coal cakes from the front door to the kitchen. Firstly, I put two coal cakes on even ground, placed a wooden board down called a washboard, a laundry board and used it to carry coal cakes. The washboard had many other functions, like wives forcing their cheating husbands to stand on it on their knees to punish them.

I lifted my washboard with fully loaded coal cakes, say twelve pieces, and carefully carried it toward the kitchen in my apartment. I made sure the dirty coal powder didn't touch my clean clothes. For lifting heavy stuff without leaning into my upper body I needed greater arm strength.

I did not need to do laundry after this heavy and dirty job. I had no energy left over to do more housework. Everyone was supposed to do his/her own laundry, including shoes and socks, kids were not excepted. Elevator? Washing machine? No! Appliances were not seen in the Cultural Revolution. The first-ever nine-inch black-and-white domestic TV set, the "Gold Star," came to my home in 1978. I watched the FIFA World Cup final game— Argentina beat the Netherlands. The first-ever Romanian refrigerator "Arctic" came to my home in about the same year. We got it from a Beijing medical supply superstore. It was sold as a medical device, not a household appliance. The laundry machine and the home telephone arrived as late as 1990. The elevator was in service in 1988.

On one occasion, the washboard in my arms was crooked and the coal cake broke into a few pieces. From then on, I had to abandon it. To substitute, I used a wooden stool. I turned it over and it became a basket with its four legs pointing up. The stool's braces and legs formed a fence, protecting the coal cake from falling out. The hardwood stool was much heavier than the washboard, and the number of coal cakes that it could carry did not increase. So, once a month, I carried 150–200 pieces of coal cake at a time. The fuel consumption was four to five full-sized coal cakes per stove per day. Have you ever seen coal ash shovels and iron bars, or the size of a set of several cast-iron furnace rings and their iron hooks? No? Then you are too young. Whoever has seen them must be older than fifty.

In the last couple of years of the Cultural Revolution there was an LPG (liquified petroleum gas) can supply. I finally skipped from the coal-cakes-lifting job. But there was another heavy-duty job for me, the 50 lbs. LPG can lift, once every month. The whole family was in action: one person to steer the bicycle, the other one, or better, two people to secure the LPG cylinder on the bicycle's rear seat. In fact, the cylinder had been tied to the back seat/rack of the bicycle. It did not help with two people on each side of the bicycle. I operated/handled it alone. I put that cylinder on the spring clip on the back shelf/rack of the bicycle without a rope, because by the time you tied it onto the rack the centre of gravity of the bicycle may be tilted, and the cylinder might fall together with the bicycle. I rode my bicycle to the exchange station. On one occasion, my cylinder fell off my bicycle rack. It rolled and rolled on the pavement of the road until it stopped in the roadside drainage ditch, where there was soft dirt/mud. It was okay by me. I smiled and picked up the cylinder, clipped it back onto my bicycle's rack and moved on. The ridiculous thing was that a few pedestrians walked by, adults and children, and they all ran away or dropped down for their lives. Nothing happened. It was an empty can. With a fully filled LPG heavy cylinder, I bicycled back to my new residence building—our home had moved from 5-110 on the ground floor to 12-303 on the third floor. I had to make my bicycle stand up straight, lock it, and carry the 70–90 lbs. heavy can upstairs to the third floor. In the stairwell there was nowhere I could find to lean the cylinder and take a break. It was full of bicycles, and useless stuff was piled up in the stairwell. I had to do this in one try, and it made me feel like a man, although I was only fifteen or sixteen.

Ordinary people do not know the difference between LPG and gas from coal. So, they followed the popular wisdom and called LPG "gas." In fact, the gas from coal is more dangerous. Its main content, carbon monoxide, is a fatal gas. I once slept away in my apartment kitchen because our coal-burning stove was incompletely burning the coal cake and releasing some carbon monoxide while

I was dishwashing after lunch. It almost cost me my life. The LPG is not dangerous. It is not even gaseous when it is in a compressed container, it is liquid. The LPG is vaporized little by little in the space above the upper surface of the LPG inside of the tank and released by a device called a regulator. This part of the gas is let out of the tank and can be set on fire or ignited. It is far away from an explosion and an out-of-control fire.

Why should I talk so much about this? You must know who I am. I am from a two-generation family of chemists. My mom and dad both were chemists, chemical professors at the Steel Courtyard. My uncles were chemical engineers. I studied chemistry as a major.

The boys had to do everything in that era. If you missed a few jobs or experiences, the labour performance on your school report would be "not good," and it would impact your ranking of the "three good students, five good soldiers." The evaluation would further affect you so that you could not join the Young Pioneers—then it was called the Junior Red Guard—in elementary school, neither could you join the Red Guards in middle school, nor the Communist Youth League in high school.

My home had a balcony. Hundreds of cabbages and sweet potatoes could be stocked there for the vegetable low season in winter and spring. With this background I could skip a job, i.e., digging a cellar. There was no need to dig a vegetable cellar for my family. I was happy too early. A labour job representative in my class reported me, and I was given an opportunity to do this job. Another classmate of mine had a similar situation and background. Coincidentally, his surname was also Cheng. Cheng Xin Ping and I took a truck, the domestic "liberation four-ton" truck, to the Sand River, 60 kilometres away from our school, to dig sand. There was a sieve in the riverbed, and we shoveled the sand to sieve it and then raised it high, throwing the finely sieved sand into the bed of the truck. In four hours, we had filled the truck with four tons of sand. Then we sat on top of the sand in the back of the truck, returned to our school, and unloaded the sand into the sandpit. On that day, we two teenagers sieved four tons of sand, loaded four tons, and unloaded four tons. What a performance! It was way beyond a teenager's energy limit.

Another point is that sitting on top of a truck fully loaded with sand is extremely dangerous. The truck driver didn't care about us. At any bump our thin bodies were thrown up lightly and dropped down heavily. Thank God we landed on the sand again and again. It was lucky that we did not smash into pieces. In the darkness we were finally home in one piece. Sand, dirt, mud—every dirty thing from the river was in our eyes, nose, mouth, ears. The exercise was finally over. We had passed this brutal test. We were never sent again to do this or similar work.

In 1983, all the students at the university were forced to plant trees and live in the desert directly outside of Beijing. We were on the final stage of writing our graduation theses, preparing for oral defense. We had to stop studying and plant trees. This is a disguised form of corporal punishment, which uses manual labour and harsh living conditions to wash away our progressively liberalized thoughts. I didn't go. There was an excuse. My graduation thesis instructor, Mr. Tan Zanlin, was a doctoral candidate at that time, and he broke his leg. He was Mr. Wei Shou Kun's first PhD disciple, and his family was in Hu Nan Province, 1000+ kilometres away from Beijing. He studied for a PhD degree in our Steel Courtyard and lived alone on fourth floor in a student dormitory. I was Mr. Tan's only disciple, so I had to help him move around, carry him up and down stairs on my back. For this good reason I successfully skipped the tree-planting labour job. A Communist party member, An Sheng Li, the branch secretary in my class, wrote and labelled me something negative in my school report; that is, I "do not like physical labor job."

Here I have two things to clear: there are classes in every single Chinese university; and in each class there is a Communist party branch. The red axes were among our university students, teachers, and professors. And in 2014, I was digging outside the walls of the Academy of Metering Sciences, not far from the Sand River. This time, my father's ashes were buried in the earth, side by side with my mother who had passed away thirteen years earlier. I wish them a good life together again in the other world.

9
Farmland or School

At the end of 1967, as the greatest leader, Mao, used the students of secondary schools and universities to win the political struggle/fight against his current or potential opponents, he as an old man came up with the words: "To resume schooling in a revolutionary course." I was seven years old. Time to go to school. And primary schools were reopened. But my school and others ran in a completely stupid way: Monday to Saturday, every day at 8:00 a.m., the first period started as the bell rang. No one dared to be late to Chairman Mao's morning request instruction time. The class stood up for worship. The class monitor took the lead, shouting: "First of all, let us wish the Great Mentor, the Great Leader, the Great Commander-in-Chief, the Great Helmsman Chairman Mao unlimited long life." We all waved his booklet in our hands four times. Four waves, twice shouting: "Long life without borders! Long life without borders!" The monitor took the lead again, shouting: "We wish the great leader Chairman Mao's closest comrade-in-arms Deputy Commander Lin good health!" We all waved Chairman Mao's booklet four times and shouted twice: "For ever good health! Forever good health!" Sing our national anthem? No! Fly our national flag? No!! We didn't have our country to love in that moment. We had Mao only. And he was everything we should be loyal to. Then we could sit down, open Chairman Mao's booklet, turn to the page the teacher instructed, read the first few lines of the paragraph, and recite Chairman Mao's quotations. We had to recite them by heart, because we were only the first graders of primary school, and we couldn't yet read Chairman Mao's quotations. We did not know how to read. We had to find some way to read his great work loudly, without any mistakes. Or, when you felt like you wanted to drop your learning course, there was a place for you to go, the farmland. Primary school was not good, secondary school was not good. Vast Chinese farmland was good. Chairman Mao had such a big mouth: "Acknowledged young people go to the countryside, to receive further education/deep study from the poor and lower-middle-class peasants. It is necessary." This call was a ruse; the original school students were with him, helping him to successes in a revolution to bring down the Communist party committees at a different level, and the public legal system, legislation system, and government at different levels. Students were fooled. They dropped off their school bags, picked up a pail and packed blankets and food containers for the countryside where they were dispersed, worked in the field, fought for their food. They could no longer assemble and form a new political powerhouse. This was the merge into peasants' farming teams, who settled down in the countryside. They lost their citizenship in towns and cities, which meant their food would not be supplied by the government, they were on their own. In the countryside, they did not have land, no properties, no homes. Their enthusiasm to follow Mao and become Axes had crashed. They were the poorest political cannon fodder thrown out by Mao.

All my elder cousins had fallen into this trick well. They left Beijing or Shanghai where the living standards were significantly better than anywhere else in China— they are even better today, for Shanxi, Shaanxi, Guizhou,

Yunnan and other poor provinces in China would show how loyal to Chairman Mao they were. Wanting to go to a slightly better place made it appear as if you were not so revolutionary, not so loyal to him.

Because they were intellectuals, they fought for power with Chairman Mao once. What if they tried it again for somebody else? So, remaining in Beijing and towns across the country was a huge threat to Mao. Mao had no rivals in Beijing. Potential rivals would emerge from students, especially student leaders. This is the politician playing with the power of the well-known proverbs: "Cross the river, then break the bridge. Mill job is done, then kill the donkey." Unfortunately, bridges and donkeys (cannon fodder) did not know these tricks. They didn't understand why their great leader treated them this way. They handed over power to the workers' Mao Ze Dong thought-propaganda team, the military representatives, and then happily responded to Chairman Mao's call to "The vast world, a great deal of action." They were decentred from the national political centre, the capital Beijing and other provincial political capital centres. As to what kind of living standard they were going to have, Mao did not care. They cared. But it was too late.

In my primary school, there were almost no students over two years older than me, because there had been no spring enrollment since 1966. The original elementary school students were all upgraded to middle school. They went to Beijing No. 93 Middle School. And students who didn't graduate from No.93 were upgraded to the attached high school of the Steel Courtyard. The three schools could not be overloaded; regardless of graduation or not, people just wrapped their things and went to the countryside. They became farmers without their own fields, without their own housing, and without food and drinks. Some of them went to Bing Tuan, which is a semi-military group located in Xin Jiang, Mongolia, and ex-Manchuria. Graduates and undergraduates emigrated to the countryside, to the minority-nation-occupied area, and stayed there until 1979. If you could not pass the national university/college entrance exams there was only way for your future to go: becoming a farmer. When we were at middle school, we were forced to sign a statement saying that we were voluntarily following Chairman Mao's call to go to the farmland. The middle-school principals and the head teachers of every class (the class sizes were fifty-plus students) took a table and let us fill it out, and we vowed to voluntarily go to the countryside and settle down there. The school sealed the forms in everybody's personal file. The file was supposed to follow his/her whole life. After 1978, the school stopped forcing its own graduates to sign such forms. Temporary workers quietly emerged. Their employer was a company subsidized by every kind of courtyard. It was called the "labor and service company." Parents' courtyards hired their adult sons and daughters as temporary workers. They were paid 1.50 yuan/day, or 45 yuan/month. They lined up for the formal recruitment of the courtyard they worked in. Forty years have passed, and dozens of us students had gone around the universities, wandering, changing jobs, going abroad, etc. The temporary workers got permanent positions to stay and work for the Steel Courtyard. They are all living a happy retired life in their hometown, the Steel Courtyard. My female classmates retired at the age of fifty-five, my male ones at sixty. Of course they were not able to do research and tuition work in this university, but they maintained the university campus, the equivalent of small-town living: gardeners, early child educators, financiers, infrastructure workers, electricians, plumbers, drivers, security officers, chefs, logistic workers, printers, property managers, even janitors, boiler operators, etc. These are contractor's jobs in Western universities. China's universities are in charge overall. No wonder a president of Tsinghua University once boasted that he was not only the president of Tsinghua University, but also the mayor of Tsinghua City/Township. Tsinghua and the Steel Courtyard were large entities, each had populations of thousands. China's large entities were something equal to miniature cities. This is an exaggeration. They let foreign experts and scholars study in China on in-depth research paths. By the way, before the Communist government was founded in 1949, this kind of place was once called a "base," like a military one, with bandits occupying the mountain as the king of the cottage. It's no different.

At school, no one can be free of campus bullying. This is a worldwide problem. China's campuses not only have bullying, but even more serious concerns. Campus bullying in China has its initiators. I think it is the parents. Parents worked in the same courtyard. Their children visited the school attached to that courtyard. The positional differences of the parents were used badly by those kids whose parents ranked higher. They were 100 percent the bullying winners, the rest of us being losers.

During the Cultural Revolution, the factor of good origin was particularly prominent, the so-called "good birth" was the children of workers, peasants, military personnel, and cadres. The origin that was not good was our teachers' children, as well as the children of the cadres who had been defeated. Born good, you go on bullying anyone. If you had a bad background then you were bullied, and this has become an unwritten rule. If you were born bad but still wanted to bully people, you were killing yourself. Chinese society has never been equal. It is hegemony. It is far away from human rights, as people are born equally. Doing anything against higher-ranked people is suicide in China. Period. I could beat my classmate easily, but his dad was my dad's big boss. I should not make trouble for my dad. Then this bullying converts. I was bullied by my classmate. I should have cried instead of fighting back, pretended I was a loser then, and forever a loser. What would have happened if I didn't care and beat him anyway? I had to pay an apology, had to write a reflection. My dad felt sorry for his boss's poor kid and he punished me at home. He had to make this punishment so loud or so effective that everybody saw it with great fear and reported it to the boss. School bullying become a domestic violation.

I threw a piece of rock and hit the eye of my primary school classmate Zhang Shi Hong. The whole school assembled in the afternoon on the same day and our vice-principal Ms. Zuo admonished me on the paging system for the whole afternoon. I survived—my dad and his were the same ranking at the university, the lecturers. His mom was my primary school teacher. Lucky me.

Another son of a gym teacher was not so lucky. Wang Yue, the son of Wang Yu Pu, a physical education teacher in intellectual class at the Steel Courtyard, punched the son of a caretaker and gave him a black eye. The victim's dad was working class. The class struggle in China in the Cultural Revolution made it clear: the working class comes first and is the winner in any challenge to any other class. Down to the earth, this one punch cost Wang Yue and his dad so heavily that they stripped them (Father Wang and his son Junior Wang) of everything. Uncle Wang was a member of the Kuomintang/National party. Wang's origin is therefore very poor; his dad was a public enemy or historical counter-revolutionist. That's the communist's mortal enemy. The punishment against the family Wang was this: day and night, whenever there was a knock on the door, there was an "emergency" call. "The victim felt not well." His elder sister the door-crasher told Wang Yue that her brother must be transported to the best hospital, the #3 attached to Beijing University Hospital immediately. Our high-ranker's car became an ambulance in the nighttime and its driver must respond to the night-duty call every time. The poor son of the worker didn't have any serious injuries but liked riding in the luxury car. When he saw from his window that the luxury car was in the garage again, he got "sick." He did not worry about the cost and the hate. Family Wang must cover all costs, no matter what. The guilty Wang Yue never raised his head up in his youth again. His fight was named "the counter-revolutionist attacked the working class," the most revolutionary class defined by Carl Max, Fredrich Engels, Vladimir Lenin, Joseph Stalin and Mao Ze Dong. And we were the intellectual class, which was the least favourite group of the Red Axes everywhere in China. The funny thing is that after the Cultural Revolution the intellectual class would join the working class actively. Their brain work is also a kind of labour work. As to the labour working class accepting this or not, who cares? We anesthetize ourselves. We were overjoyed at being the first class in China, although we were far from it. Workers are overjoyed at being the first class in China, although they are not. The real first class in China is the Red Axes.

The ingenious bully not only beat people to bully a weak classmate, but also wantonly destroyed their books, stationery, bicycles, etc., and smashed and robbed public property, verbally abused male teachers, teased female teachers, beat principals, ganged up on other schools to group fight. At Tsinghua University, students with trouser belts beating "class position problem" teachers were a typical scenario. They kidnapped the teacher in a room with a plywood board nailed to the window. There was an electric lamp. Soon after, the head of the Axe came into the room and found his torture object, the teacher. He was already tied up and kneeling on the floor so that he couldn't move. Before he recognized who was going to bully him, the head of the Axes swung his belt and put out the light. The room went dark. He then belt-whipped this poor teacher. Both ends of his belt had a metal buckle. When they hit the teacher at this whipping speed, there was screaming, struggling, and screaming like an animal being attacked. This belt was so popular during the Cultural Revolution that from then on everybody in China knew that this kind of belt was a fatal device when torturing was going on. The screaming/crying boomed all over the corridor, and even spread to the outside for the first several minutes. Then there was silence. Did the poor teacher pass out, or did he die of pain and his blood being drained off? I do not know. Such victims were classified as "bull, ghost, snake, and evil." Their crying was supposed to be this way. Was there any other way?

In the hallway, there were other tied-up people, or "bull, ghost, snake, and evil," waiting for their turns to be belt-whipped. They were shocked and shuddering. That was and is the Red Axes struggling against their class enemies. Hitler beat his enemies in the concentration camps and prisons. Stalin killed his enemies in the secret places. But the Red Axes all over China beat their enemies on Mao's behalf directly on the university campuses, in the residence buildings, and sometimes directly in the street. So, who is more evil? These brutal tactics are still going on in China, in Xin Jiang, in Tibet, in Hong Kong. In North Korea. Who knows if they do these bad things publicly or secretly? In China, people get tortured by Red Axes publicly. It is an open bullying place for free. Period.

In the Steel Courtyard, students and young teachers who used to be like my father and other middle-aged teachers' students tortured my father and other "problematic and refusing to confess" people. Here again I mention the torture against my father. He was banged against an steel shelf. The Axe who tortured him grabbed his hair and knocked his head against the bunk bed. This torture made my father's brain damaged. His memory was greatly reduced, and his logical ability was almost lost. A man who went to two of the country's top universities, Tsinghua University and Peking University, who once so proudly showed off his ability of analysis and his excellent memory, now had a wounded brain, it was over.

Dozens of people were suffering similar tortures at the same time. They were silent. I am not. In my high school years, I wrote it into a composition. The title of the proposition essay is "My Father." With my pen, my father had just come out of his cell where he had been unlawfully detained and came home with tears in his eyes. "You don't want to be a teacher." Mr. Huang He (Yellow River), my Chinese language teacher, gave me a score of A+, which is excellent. He was also a victim of the Cultural Revolution. Because of his born talent that came from Si Chuan Province, or "Ba Shu" area naturally, the Republic of China and the Kuomintang/National party hired him as a newspaper editor during the anti-Japanese War. He edited for pro-KMT newspapers. Yellow River is either his real name or a fake name, we never knew. He passed my work to my father. According to my mother, my father cried and cried after reading this work. Nobody could persuade him to stop crying.

So long as my memory and logical analysis is still alive today, I will force myself to recall those events and details as much as possible. And publish them all. I do to never imitate the faults and crimes of these predecessors in the world and beyond. Study history, don't just copy it. Don't repeat history. After being beaten, my father lost his dignity and the courage to live. He somehow sneaked out of his cell, ran away from the Steel Courtyard, and went to the fifth railway intersection nearby, where he walked around waiting for a passing train to come, and he was ready to lie down and kill himself. That day was long. He didn't see a train coming. Instead, he saw a man walking back and forth, too. It seemed like he was also waiting for a passing train, seeking to kill himself on the tracks. Isn't that Ke Jun? Mr. Ke Jun was a high-end scientist that Premier Zhou Enlai called back to China from the United Kingdom, right after 1949, when the Communist party conquered China. Mr. Ke was a research fellow of the Chinese Academy of Sciences who worked in the Steel Courtyard. He had an official scientific assistant/secretary. And that assistant was my dad. Ke Jun had two majors that made him number one in the world: the history of metallurgy and metallography.

When they met in the middle of the railway station, they knew what they were going to do next: commit suicide. Everyone's situation was about the same. The Red Axes tortured them, humiliated them, stripped off their dignity and made them feel like they were in the wrong time, living in the current world. What a country they were living in. The Red Axes had the right to do anything, regardless of right or wrong, while the intellectuals could not do anything. Everything they thought was wrong. Everything they tried was wrong. Their background judged this right/wrong, not the fact. This is against their belief: the experiment/fact is the paramount judge of science. They would rather die. The two intellectuals met on the midway of nowhere, speechless for nobody knows how long. Then they made up their minds to not die that day. They must continue their lives, even though their lives were not as good as a dog's in that moment. So, they returned to the Steel Courtyard as if nothing happened. Thank God. The trains passed that railway twice every day during the Cultural Revolution. They didn't know the schedule, or they didn't stay there long enough. They continued to be interrogated by torture, and all the things they confessed were fabricated, and the timing and locations did not match the role they played. It wasn't true. So that's how they survived that ten-year-long Cultural Revolution.

This was campus bullying, in which students tortured each other, insulted their teachers, professors, deans, principals—including world-class master Ke Jun and his assistant, my father, who was a top-ranked youth teacher and potentially promoted sooner and higher than other jealous people.

In 1978, Mr. Ko regained some power in the Steel Courtyard, and he would first send my father to West Germany, to have a look at universities in the Western World. My father was forty-seven years old then. Going back to school really turned him on. He was trying hard to get a chance to study abroad at the age of seventeen.

The first tryout was not there; his score only qualified him to go to the Peking University. A year later in 1948 he tried out again and this time his score was high enough to go to the TsingHua University. Tsinghua is American founded as a preparation school to the U.S. The door was opened to my dad to study in the U.S., but the timing was wrong. The communists in China closed the door to the U.S., to Europe, and to the Western World. The Communist party came, and studying abroad meant that they could only go to East Bloc countries, the best one being the Soviet Union, followed by East Germany, Czech and Slovakia, Bulgaria, Yugoslavia, Albania, Poland, North Korea and Cuba, etc. There were no exams to write. The decision of who could study abroad was made by the Communist committees in the universities.

For my father, this was a dead-end to going anywhere. His dad, my grandfather, was not in the Red Axes' class. This could not bring them, father and son, even grandson, any benefits. My dad would have been better to stay and study at Tsinghua. But his dream was broken again: he studied in the Tsinghua chemistry department. There was an adjustment of faculties between Tsinghua and Peking universities among others in 1950. His chemistry faculty in Tsinghua was moved completely to the department of chemistry at the Peking University. The Axes wanted Tsinghua to be an engineering school and Peking University to be an academic school. So, he had to move back to Peking University to continue his studies. In 1952, my father finished his four-year university course and was assigned to work at the Institute of physical chemistry, Chinese Academy of Sciences in Chang Chun City, Ji Lin province, where it was Manchuria. Because he was too active at university, he was the human resource minister of the student union in Tsinghua (the president of the student alumni was Zhu Rong Ji, who later became a right-winger against Mao in 1957 for twenty years, and later became a prime minister in 1994 for more than ten years), and later my dad was the performing arts minister of the student alumni at Peking University. He was appointed as a team leader of five graduates by Peking University and reported to the director of the Changchun Institute of Physical Chemistry, with four other university graduates assigned to Changchun. These five were supposed to work all their lives in Chang Chun City, but the director firstly conducted a political review. Four out of five graduates were Chinese Communist party members. The only non-party guy was my dad, and he was their leader! This was unacceptable. I am not sure if all the party members were Red Axes, but I am quite sure that non-party members had no chance to be Axes—even their leadership skills were higher. So, the director sent my father back to Peking University—a rejection! My dad got a dismissal from his job before he started to work, because and only because he was not a Communist! He left the four Communist party member graduates to work for the glorious party behind.

Peking University had to send my father for a second time, this time to the newborn Steel Courtyard in Beijing. Here the political orientation was not as straightforward as in the Chinese Academy of Science. He went into the Steel Courtyard, where he worked for a lifetime. The other four people who stayed and worked in Changchun complained about my father for all their lives as the living standard in Beijing was getting better and better, the central seat of centralism. Changchun was getting worse and worse; the worst time Changchun citizens experienced was in the Cultural Revolution when the military's regional commander, Chen Xi Lian, and political committee Chief, Mao Zedong's nephew Mao Yuan Xin, held the power, which meant they were emperors or rulers to three provinces with populations of close to 100 million in Northeast China. Among immigrants from all over China to Manchuria, they got 150 grams/person or 150 millilitres of vegetable oil a month only (meanwhile, citizens from other places could get 250 grams of vegetable oil a month) as citizens. As to farmers, they got zero or north–west wind only. Commander Chen had been called "Chen San-Liang." 150 milli-litre oil is about "san Liang" in Chinese Metrics.

The logistics chain was not there for about two to three years, until October 1976 when the 10th Marshal Ye Jian Ying took down the Gang of Four, including Mao's widow Jiang Qing. And Mao's nephew was arrested. In 1983, my schoolmate from Northeast China told me about the hard days in their hometown: not enough vegetable oil, their cooking way was to creatively get to the rednecks' level—cooking vegetables with boiling water instead of oil. After cooking, dip a chopstick in water, then dip the water-coated chopstick into the oil bottle, and then stir the cooked vegetables. It should be called "dressing." The new way of cooking was called "the second-wife oiling." The oil level in the oil bottle did not drop but rose because the water underneath got deeper. More water in the oil bottle lifts the oil level.

The greater the living-standard difference between Beijing and Changchun, the harder they complained. It was almost like my dad pitied them. Then the reward came to me. In 1986 I graduated. Although I was assigned to stay and work in Beijing, I was not to skip the one whole year "social practice" for each graduate student and post-graduate student. Somebody played a role as a pit, and he was my classmate, and the Communist party chief in our post-graduate student class. Watch the difference here, Chinese schools vs. schools elsewhere in the world: each grade had a class or classes, and in each class, there was a Communist party representative and a class head teacher. This system existed in all schools, including engineering schools, art schools, language schools, political party schools, and applied to all grades, including post-doctorate. The party's network spread out everywhere systematically. The Red Axes over China, I mean.

The party chief in my class got the same job as I did: young teacher. He signed up to go for the social practice for a year first, ahead of anybody else who got the same offer at the same school we just graduated from. The pit was formed. I was the first one to follow him, and I signed up. I was in the pit. Then I had to go. He did not have to go. There was a deal under the table which I did not know about. All the party-member graduates knew. The place I had to go to was China at the Soviet Union border area. I served there for one school year from August 1986 to July 1987.

Come back and read the story of my father and Mr. Ke Jun. The Cultural Revolution was over in Oct. 1976. Ko asked the Steel Courtyard to promote my father. A professor's title was unnegotiable. A deputy one was OK. Ke needed a professor to sign an official agreement of partnership on his behalf with the Aachen Tech University in West Germany. My father should have been this signing officer. The promotion was perfect. My father got one complete year off from his duties at his university to learn the ABCs of the German language, followed by a two-year-long trip to West Germany to inspect the university in Aachen and sign the partnership agreement if everything was OK. What a return this was, from being suicidal together with your highly intelligent boss to changing his mind, as well as your own? This once-a-year

German language course cured my father's persistent memory problem, which had led to a broken memory. A year later, in 1979, my dad went to West Germany as a private representative of Professor Ke and a mini-group of the Steel Courtyard. Of course, the leader of this mini-group was not my dad but a communist representative Ms. Wang Xiu Mei. In line, I also successfully entered the Steel Courtyard as a university rooster. To make my dad happier, I would study directly in my father's profession, physical chemistry for metallurgy. My original favourite major was and is literature/creative writing, but I feared Chinese literature—the Red Axes were still over China. As a writer one can easily become a current counter-revolutionist and not have a bright future. To be an engineer is much safer. Even when an engineer makes mistakes in his design, forgets this, misses that, it will be fine. Being politically correct is not so sensitive when you're a career engineer.

There was double happiness coming home: I went to study at a regular/focused university and my dad went to study abroad. His dream came true. But wait a moment. Germany and maybe the whole world knew then that Chinese students tortured their teachers in the Cultural

Revolution in China. When my dad and other Chinese students showed up in their classroom, e.g. to learn the German language, the language teacher refused them. "What if the Chinese students come into my classroom and belt whip me?"

You see, the bullying was so bad. It was my dad again, standing up and telling the world that we were victims, too. My father reminded me again and again before he went to Germany that he and I should behave in this period. No one should cause any trouble. And I had already thought about going to fight school bullying, to try it out at least. Fortunately, my father stopped me.

After two years or so, the school broadcast station announced "good news": Mr. Ke Jun became a new member of the Communist party after a long-term application. All the students laughed at him. He was sixty-five in that year. And we university students were experiencing faithless crises in that time. In the same year, Mr. Ko's scientific assistant, my father, was sent back to the Steel Courtyard. His faculty Communist party chief, his former student and current colleague, Ms. Duan Shu Zhen, convinced him to join the Communist party. She said that my father had fulfilled all requirements the party had set up for intellectuals in China. My father was not funny like his academic boss, Mr. Ke Jun. He replied that he would withdraw his application for joining the Communist party, because his trip to Germany had given him a change of faith.

The next year, in 1983, Professor Lin Zong Cai of the metallurgical department of the Steel Courtyard pulled my dad into another party, the Chinese Democratic Union, or CDU in short. It had the same three letters as the German political party CDU, which has held power for decades in Germany. I can mention two great leaders in that German party: Angela Merkel and Helmut Kohl. Back to the Chinese CDU. Professor Lin Zong Cai's brother or cousin, Mr. Lin Xiang Qian, was a martyr who died during the "Feb. 7 Great Strike" of the Beijing-HanKou Railway in 1923. It was the first-ever Chinese railway-worker strike. Prof. Lin's wife, known as Mrs. Lin or Big Sister Lin, also had the surname Lin. Lin Xiang Qian was one of Lin's brothers for sure. More detail I do not know. It doesn't matter, their son was my "big head brother," and was a few years older than I was. The Cultural Revolution delayed his school time, I came to make it up. I also became a remedial teacher. In the resident building #12, unit 302, lived Liu Xiaojiang's family of six. She was my classmate in middle school/high school. In her family's two-bedroom apartment I completed the first-ever tutor hour of my life. My students were Ms. Liu and my "big head brother" Lin. It was in the first half of 1979. My father started his political career with the Chinese CDU in 1983. I continued. In the beginning of 1989, I joined CDU. In a new member greeting summit I gave a speech. In that speech I could foresee that there would be a democratic wave in China. It did came in April, May, and June in Beijing, 1989, but sadly ended up with a bloody military crash-down.

In the Chinese CDU, my father followed CDU Chairman Fei Xiao Tong. Mr. Fei was the representative/spokesperson of all eight democratic parties in China. Within the Democratic party or between the democratic parties there was fair play. Over top of these eight parties was the Chinese Communist party, the Red Axes. They bullied the eight democratic parties. Example: during Mr. Fei's term of chairman of the CDU, he had to report to the Communist party minister of the united front, Minister Yan Ming Fu. Why must other independent party chiefs listen to the Communist party minister? Are there truly politically independent parties in China? No. The communist minister Yan was the emperor of the eight democratic parties. Such facts you will also find in the other communist colonies—East Germany, the Soviet Union, Poland, etc. As a matter of fact, all democratic parties in the ex-East-Bloc were vase parties. This is another sense of bullying: political bullying. The bullying is a concrete manifestation of the communist united front chief forcing democratic parties to write explicitly in the first of their own party constitutions—the party, the alliance, or the society—that their party must support the Communist party and follow its leadership. In China, these eight parties were founded earlier than 1949 when Mao declared his new People's Republic of China. No political parties were permitted thereafter. In the vase parties, the heads were obviously getting old, unwilling to surrender to or challenge the Communist party's united front minister, the new rich. They had as little dignity as usual. They were ordinary people, too. As a result, my father would have to deal with the communist minister at his secretarial level, the deputy level. The Communist party minister of the united front had a multiple chart, from its central committee to local, and to the institutes like the Steel Courtyard. My poor dad had to surrender/ report to every single united front minister at all levels. These united front ministers, high and low rankers, from the central to the local, were the real bullies who had been bullying our faith and political preference. The Red Axes over China have always had the right to bully.

10

Street Violence: Scolding the Street

Here's some of the violence in the streets during the Cultural Revolution: scolding the streets, wandering the streets, burning cars and set-up bullying.

The street is usually a showcase of women, others are just onlookers, and a wonderful place to get a good laugh. Spicy girls were loud enough to make everybody quiet. Most people were the audience. The more of an audience there was, the spicier the spicy girls were. One woman could perform several hours of monologue drama, with all dirty words, without repeated words. We called her a language expert in the scolding category. Scolding but fighting. This could turn into an entertaining show to all the kids. The cutting edge/advanced scolding was as follows:

"I am better/stronger than you are? Don't you know?"

"You are the wall! You're all walls except the fence!"

Clever use of the same kind of diaphonemic characters, strong and wall, the other side from everyone's favouring of the strong suddenly turning into everyone hating the brick wall. High-level scolding.

"You get out!"

"Roll on. Roll eggs, roll duck eggs, roll out a grenade, kill you, bitch!"

The pair turned two eggs into grenades. Low-skilled scolding.

Guo Wen Gui and/or Miles Guo, playing live broadcasts in recent years, quoted a street-word scolding: "Put your lap farts!" But there's something different from the folk proverb. My version is: "Put your radish esthetic, snobs!" A radish esthetic fart is more inexplicable; miseating radishes resulting in non-stop farting is closer to daily life. If you are a healthy person and you eat a radish and then drink hot tea, it will guarantee that you will keep farting. An elegant statement is "reflux gas," or the idiom sling is "in the intestines of the fart." More seriously, one will have a food-poisoning phenomenon. You will need to see a doctor or go to the hospital in an ambulance.

"Eat radish, drink hot tea, so angry doctor crawled all over the street." The nursery rhymes prohibit improper food pairing to prevent food poisoning, and they contribute a great amount.

The inclusion of nursery rhymes and folk proverbs in the section of street scolding seems inappropriate and reduces the name of the first two. But I'm going to write more in order to earn more manuscript fees, so write them together for more readers to read. If I write them separately but get less readers, I earn less.

"I assure the great leader Chairman Mao that something has happened to Vice-Commander Lin." It was true. Several of our children hid in the bomb shelter that had been completed near our homes and listened to a boy a few years older than us.

Soon after, U.S. Secretary of State Dr. Kissinger visited China and brought in some American journalists. The people of the whole country had made full preparations for a response in order to recruit these enemies, the Americans, and the official demand was not to be humble.

"If Americans greet you, say 'hello!' you should answer, 'You low, me too low.'" Of course, this is a folk version.

The Americans seemed to hear that something was wrong with Lin Biao and asked everyone they met in the street what happened to Vice-Commander Lin. The answer was, "Go pee!" The word was not in the Xinhua dictionary, nor in the Kangxi dictionary, but it was difficult to bring down the Americans. "Go pee" is Chinese slang. All of China knows that "Go pee, catch cold, big malus" means death, but also the death of the deceased's disrespectful expression. Of course, this is also a folk version. My works rarely have official articles/chapters, but many slang terms. The purpose is for grassroot readers to understand China in an easy way.

Directly scold "your mother B" is serious, or pure dirty words. The Steel Courtyard had a child named Wang Gen, whose father worked at Qinghe Steelworks, and had little money for his alcoholic addiction. He often called his son to buy bulk liquor, 0.13 yuan/50 ml. Watch for this: China has freedom, too. Kids can buy alcohol. "Genlo, 2 Liang. (100 ml spirit, 53 percent–65 percent alcohol in it!" was Wang Gen's father's order. Wang Gen was a good-tempered boy, everyone shouted "Genlo" at him, but he never got angry. Soon, his father's golden sentence was popular again, first in the Steel Courtyard and then throughout the whole country. The father-son conversation of the year was:

"Dad! Buy me a pair of shoes."

There was no money for that. The dad was speechless.

"Dad! Buy me a pair of shoes," Genlo begged.

"Buy your mother's leg!" his dad roared.

This "your mother's leg" has since replaced the poisonous "your mother B." Today's live broadcast is still singing during the swearing. This is written proof. We made coarse language milder.

Later, a family from a province moved into the #5 resident building of the Steel Courtyard in Beijing. A lovely little boy started playing with us. We didn't bully him but copied his foreign accent. He was catching up on Beijing children, saying "your mother B" in his funny accent: "Your mother Gay!" From then on, the happy children of the Steel Courtyard substituted "Ma B" with the newly created "Ma Gay." This made the extremely coarse language change to the funniest word. And we were too young to learn what on earth "gay" meant. Today, scolding is no longer directly scolding mom, but sister instead, "Take care of your sister, eh!" and "Brush your sister!" And so, language is also evolving; Chinese people greeting other people's old or older women gradually became a greeting to their sister, knowing that the one-child-per-family policy made their scolding safe. Most young Chinese do not have sisters at all.

11

Street Violation 11: Shame Parade

A shame parade is very negative bullying. It was popular in the Cultural Revolution. Almost every one of us saw it then. At the beginning of the Cultural Revolution, Wang Guangmei, the wife of Chinese president Liu Shaoqi, was a victim of a shame parade organized by students from Tsinghua University, and they began to roam the streets. When Wang was in the street, her necklace became a string of ping-pong balls. She had a master's degree in physics, and she was the first lady. The ordinary people learned all high rankers' privacies once they took part in such a shame parade. The Red Axes painted ugly makeup on their victim's faces, gave them ugly dresses also, and scandals, privacies exposed, etc. were all open to the public.

In the course of the shame parade, people/Red Axes thought they had the right to abuse their victims. They scolded the victims, insulted them, nullified the victims by spilling, pissing, black inking, etc. These people were committing crimes without knowing that what they were doing was illegal. They found out every fantasy, mostly ugly, to show how revolutionary they were, and had no qualms about counter-revolution. There were also some thieves and hooligans. When they get caught, people put them in a shame parade before turning them over to the police. When a female teacher or a female cadre found herself in the middle of a shame parade her dignity was destroyed by having a pair of used shoes hung around her neck. So "used shoes" has become their exclusive unified title, and "used shoes" is not limited to young women. In 2013 I returned to my dad's home to celebrate my father's 82th, birthday, and in the morning to accompany him to the big playground of the Steel Courtyard in the name of "early exercise." In fact, nobody at his age was going to do any sports, instead they only got together to chat. Old colleagues, old friends, to prove to each other that they were still alive. A ninety-year-old cadre who was one of the new Fourth Army South China column members rushed out. "That used shoes! What does she say?" They all knew that he meant Hillary Clinton, the secretary of state of the United States. He scolded her in front of a group of old Chinese people. But I didn't know. I asked around and got laughed at. A beautiful day began with a silly joke about an American woman. Jokes and good news kept the old-man group active day after day. Their bodies cannot do any exercise but they could have mind refreshment. Keeping everyone happy was the best result. They survived shame parades across the street or around the big playground of the Steel Courtyard during the Cultural Revolution. They were now having fun with each other—who was crying in the parade against him, who was kneeling in embarrassment in front of Red Axes.

I shifted the topic more vulgarly to give them a bit of fun, describing a fulfillment for marriage for a girl in Shanghai today. It is called "three 180s." The dean of the physics institute was in on the joke. He was my thermodynamics teacher, Professor Lan Zhi Bin. He asked for details. The first 180, I said, is when the man has a 180-square-metre house, and has already paid off all the mortgage and the girl won't save every cent to pay the mortgage and cut back on food, eat instant noodles, to save money for the mortgage. The second 180 is the man's height. He must be 180 cm or taller. This is to ask that, after marriage, the girl could proudly show her husband around to her relatives and friends. To marry a short man in China means the girl loves his money. She would be involved in a shame-managed marriage. According to Chinese single women, they define a 170-cm-tall man as semi-disabled, and a 160-cm-tall man as totally disabled. So, size matters. The third 180 is in millimetres—I looked at my physics professor, Mr. Lan. "You are a physics teacher, you know the scale of dimension." Professor Lan laughed. His face turned red, indicating that he understood my silly jokes. Other people turned to him, asking what was so funny.

12

Street violence III: Burning a Car

During the Cultural Revolution, a luxury car was burned at the East Hua Gate in Beijing.

From my grandparents' house out of the milky hutong, now called Kang Jian Hutong, and then out to the lamp market road, turning south to a larger street. It is the top commercial zone in Beijing, called Wangfujing. Before you hit Wangfujing, there is an intersection called Wangfujing Donghua Gate intersection. Here the road is particularly wide; the officials of the feudal dynasty got into the Forbidden City to see their emperor from here. If they rode horses, they would have to get off horseback here. And the horses were sent to the royal guest stable. In the stables they had everything: drinks, hay, a shoe-iron workshop, even ice cubes. Pets, if they were any, were divided into indoor and outdoor ones. Horses were of course the first favourite outdoor pets. Cats are the first favourite indoor pets. Dogs are a kind of crossover pet, good for outdoor, good for indoor, too. This is another agenda.

We're talking about cars and burning them. Cars are the modern horses. Tell me when I am wrong.

To burn a car there in the new era is a clear message delivered to classes/communities at large, the high rankers in the seventeen-year-young China are no different than an emperor's slave officials. During the Cultural Revolution and ten years after, senior officials were dedicated to transportation, a symbol of power. By burning it, you clearly get a signal: this revolution is against the high rankers. Mao would call it Chinese hegemonism. He was the emperor, everybody else was his slave/minister, regardless of whether he is a high ranker or a peasant. As a little boy of six, I was particularly excited to describe the ignition/burning process, but I hope readers like you don't imitate it. Learn history and don't imitate it.

Behind the rear seats of the car was a triangular space by the rear window. A duster was often placed there. Most dusters for a regular household are long handled but with short, functional heads. A car duster is the opposite:

short-handled with a long feather part. The Red Axes kicked out the driver and his passenger in the daytime, smashed the side window of the car and took out the duster. They wanted to turn the duster into a match for making a fire on the car. First a Red Axe put the duster into the car's fuel tank, dipping it in some gasoline. Then another one lit it. It was inserted into the car through the broken side window. The car seat's fabric and the cushion material inside it caught on fire, then the gasoline tank below was on fire—it was more "firewood." The inside and outside of the car were turned into a flame ball. Black smoke rose into the blue sky. In less than half an hour, the car was completely scrapped. You see, the cost of a box of matches was two cents, but it burned, destroyed a much more expansive car. It caused much air pollution, scrap-car tow-away, etc. It went to a scrap-metal junk yard. How much was it? Estimated a hundred thousand. The most unforgivable thing was that the man who ignited the car had run away free, without being charged. Did the revolution give him the power to burn cars? Yes.

At the beginning of the Cultural Revolution, a group of Red Guards came to the parliament to capture Premier Zhou Enlai, who worked there. This was also street violence. Pity it was blocked by gun guards in Zhongnanhai. In that violence there was Mr. He Shimin, who later became the director of my office, the office of the Environmental Central Supervisory Station of the Ministry of Coal Industry, China. His "glorious deeds" were packed into his file bag so he could not go abroad. He failed every political review because of this and was disqualified. Politically unqualified people do not go abroad. His position in a technical delegation in Austria was substituted by another mean person, the very man to disqualify Mr. He Shimin's political review. And his name is Li Zhonghe. Who was Li Zhonghe? He was the Communist party branch chief in our environmental station, a standard Red Axe. He was mean to me in regarding my political review, too.

In January 1989, when it was my turn to go abroad, Mr. Li Zhonghe voluntarily blocked my way out of China by disqualifying my political review. It was four-month block. In April, May, and June 1989, Beijing and China were in a sensational pro-democratic campaign. The political climate was uncertain. Taking an opportunity to go abroad was optimized. Li was in my way, blocking me.

Somebody else appeared to me like an angel. She was from Mongolia Baotou Steelworks. She came to Beijing to accompany her husband, who was promoted from Baotou to Beijing, from a nationally run enterprise at the Baotou Steelworks to the ministry of metallurgy in China. Mrs. Wang must have had an official position in Beijing, as she was in Baotou. Lucky for me, she took the director's position in my environmental station. Her ranking was just one level higher than the blocker, Mr. Li. She came into my office and asked me very politely if there was anything she could do for me. My office was my chemical lab, my computer room, and my residence room, three in one in the building that Mr. He Shimin designed and built. It was demolished by Li Zhonghe during the bureaucratic war between Li and He. There was no winner in that war. Mr. Li had a stroke. Mr. He passed away. Mrs. Wang stayed in my place on that day until she passed me on my political review, which enabled me to go abroad. My angel got her chance to go abroad, too, after she retired. Now she enjoys her happy retirement in Australia. I appreciate her so much; without her kindly clearing my last block I could have been gunned down in the bloody military crackdown on the Tiananmen Square, which was on June 4, 1989, that shocked the whole world. I took an international train from Beijing, the capital of China, to Moscow, the capital of the Soviet Union, fleeing to my destination, Aachen, West Germany. Had it not been for the timely political review of Director Wang sending me abroad, I would still have been in Beijing. Perhaps the jailed one would not be Liu Zizi and Su Gang, but me, Cheng Xun.

Flashbacks. In April 1989, Beijing university students once again rushed to the parliament and tried to get in, with typical street violence, but again failed. Somebody was beaten. If the death of the ex–Communist Party chief Mr. Hu Yaobang was the trigger, then this charge should be an igniter. Soon after April 21st, 1989, it developed into the magnificent 8964 pro-democratic protest (code name for the June 4 massacre), the big wildfire. In June 1989, cars were set on fire in the streets of Beijing again, and it was just like the event in 1966 in Beijing—it was a purely iconic political event. Most of the vehicles that were victims of the atrocity were military. It was a bunch of military vehicles going to Tiananmen Square, the political centre of Beijing, the country's political center, in peacetime; it didn't make sense. Liu, the leader of the

Steel Courtyard co-op store, was thrown in prison for adding some garbage onto a burning military vehicle. It constituted a street-violence crime. In the Steel Courtyard #5 residence unit 207, a young student, Su Gang, was also sentenced for taking part in the 8964 pro-democratic protest. These two are people I know, who lived in the same courtyard and even used the same gate.

Understandably, they're in jail for me. From a hunger strike to the end of May in 1989 I was in the Beijing streets nightly. The news from the prison was very positive. An old policeman came to a press conference to speak. Some parents of the prisoners were also invited. "8964 prisoners get the double courtesy of other prisoners and custodies." This is a sequel to say honour them as fake thugs, real heroes. Sooner or later they will be out and free. That's what I said. But the brutal fact is, as I write this chapter in May 2019, thirty years have gone by. There is no chance of turning it over, and the implementation of new policies. During 8964 the tanks were on the street, too. But there was no tank burned. This is perhaps because the Communists build their tanks so massive, or perhaps people there do not know how to set tanks on fire. Diesel-powered tanks cannot be ignited without a wick. You need wicks. The chicken-feather duster dipped with diesel won't help. Violence begins with burning cars in the streets, with extreme violence in military tanks, bloody crackdowns on civilians to stop a pro-democratic movement. Tanks rolled into the capital, Beijing, in the national political centre, to the most politically sensitive/ iconic location, in Tiananmen Square, in Chang'an Street, packed with people protesting in the streets. Driving tanks into the crowd is the worst street violence. The author has little insight and has not seen it, but I have heard of similar street violence in Lhasa, the capital of Tibet. I heard of the crackdown of the Prague Spring. But I as the author firmly believe that the perfect defeat for violence is not more violence, but something non-violent. The author cites only 8964, before and after the two cases: 1986 on the streets of Manila, the Philippine capital, gun-armed soldiers were inspired by God, tearing off the armbands of the presidential guard they were wearing, turning their muzzles and supporting the citizens, which led to the ouster of dictator President Marcos in exile. The Soviet Union began in April 1917, when a destroyer warship fired its cannon into the Winter Palace. The era ended up in 1991, when the Soviet Red Army rolled its tanks to Moscow to crush the citizens' anti-communism movement. No cannons were fired. Instead, the tank was stepped under the feet of Yeltsin. The tankman's heart was conquered by the idea of peaceful revolution against communism. Humans have really evolved and civilized. It is emphasized here that a person who possesses the means of violence, wherever he is, and who insists on the use of violence is a coward, and it takes greater courage to abandon it. We're now looking into June 9th, through Sept.29th, 2019 and weekend protests thereafter, on the streets of Hong Kong, where a peaceful march took place for millions of people. On the eve of this, some people ignited incendiary petrol bombs, changed the peace operation to street violence, for the Chinese Communist party to carry out another violent repression. Hey Red Axes! Were you the igniters? To date, the protesters in the Hong Kong Airport stopped their actions. This stopping in mid-August in 2019 in Hong Kong beats the protesters in Beijing in May 1989. The Beijinger could not stop. In challenging the communist dictatorship, Chinese people become progressively smarter.

13
Street Violence IV: Set-up Bullying

Group fights often end peacefully and rarely end in violence. I'm a bit reluctant to count the group fight as street violence. However, the uncertainty of the development of the scene of each group fight makes people extremely excited to watch. The ultimate fight is no fight. The two sides shake hands and talk. Usually one party is in the "JiangHu" underworld and his name is ranked higher than the other side is, or at the same level but from a different generation. JiangHu has its own rules. Underworld also has the epics. I should call it set up bullying.

When I was in middle-school, the only group fight that occurred was the Steel Courtyard child Wang Jin vs. the child of the geographic courtyard. In response to Chairman Mao's call during the Cultural Revolution, the geographic Institute moved from Beijing to Hubei Province. The people who remained in place did not keep the attached elementary school and the middle school running. The leftover kids in the geographic courtyard came to the nearby school to study. Too few people, too many vacancies in their courtyard. Other institutes moved in to occupy the vacant residence buildings among school classrooms and office and lab buildings. Their kids joined the group of the geographic institutes' kids. We called them all "the geo kids." This is the background.

As quests when they had to visit our school attached to the Steel Courtyard, they were supposed to behave. We the Steel Courtyard kids were the majority and we had much stronger parents. We thought that even Mao was on our side. He was the one who promoted the steel-making industry to get ready for wars. We won several rounds of bullying. Then there was a boy called Gu Jin Zhu from the geo kids' group. The vice principal of our school, Mr. Xie Guo Dong, who forced teenager girl students to work in the muddy rice-planting field and the head teacher in our class, encouraged Gu to come out and make a noise like a clown. Why can he fool around and others can't? Originally, he had a brother called Gu Jin Zhong. Gu and

Xie befriended each other in their semi-military terms in Mongolia. Xie had power now to promote Gu's younger brother, my classmate Gu Jin Zhu. The vice principal, Xie GuoDong, set up Gu Jin Zhu as a root-model of those people, who came from behind and led the class, grades, and the school. Gu was giving a speech at a school assembly, a funny version of how he could learn and apply Mao Ze Dong thought actively and flexibly.

This promotion of the geo kids caused jealousy in several children from the Steel Courtyard. The first one was Luo Jian Guo. He slapped Gu Jin Zhu's face in front of the whole class in the big playground when we were doing morning exercises, because of his lateness being laughed at by the new root-model Gu Jin Zhu. After the incident, Luo handed in a review/reflection, and the draft of his review/reflection was from another child from the Steel Courtyard. That was me. My writing skills had begun to show up, but I did not know how to use them in the right way. Then there was another teenager, Wang Jin from the Steel Courtyard, who challenged Gu Jin Zhu to a set up bullying. Wang and Gu did not dogfight right away. The two of them did not show up at school at the same time for many days. They hired fighters from JiangHu to bully at school. The two scheduled a time and place to go; that is, the woods between the Steel Courtyard–attached elementary school, the west side and #9 resident building. It was a conventional battleground where we bullied, and now it was a station for retired employees of the Steel Courtyard, a kind of community centre. The author also did very bad things there and injured his classmate Zhang Shihong. Originally it was not a fight, but the two sides automatically divided into two rows on our way home for lunch. We threw rocks at each other. My first pitch hit my classmate, Huang Chun Lei. Then I hit Zhang Shihong in the eye. He was not in the group fight, but just walking by. This is the second time he has been mentioned in this book for being wounded by me. I sincerely apologize again. Also, on the same battlefield, a nephew beat his uncle. These two were both my classmates, living in the same building, #16 residence. That building was designed and built as the largest and the last dormitory in the Steel Courtyard for the university students before the Cultural Revolution started, but no student was living in it. All rooms were put in use as residence for staff.

The younger son of a Steel Courtyard chef, Wang Yonggang, the nephew, was beating his uncle Wang

Guozheng, the first son of another Steel Courtyard chef. The former knew a few tricks of Chinese martial arts, and he liked to show them. His uncle didn't know these tricks. He then had no other choice but to become a sandbag in a Chinese martial arts show. It was my middle-school time.

Flashback to my elementary school time: Wang Yonggang kicked our common classmate Li Xuan's head here. This brutal kick made Wang the number one at our school in respect of bullying. And this kick made Li the number one most intelligent boy from our school. He is now a medical professor at Peking University. His major is fixing human brains. You never know what will result from a school bullying. The victim of the bullying, Li, is one of the extreme examples. Perhaps he is the only lucky one. How many victims of bullying are not so lucky, and they still suffer from their injuries, physical and mental?

Here also, a teacher scolded my schoolmate Chen Jiyue into tears. It happened so seldom in the Cultural Revolution. More often the student was the winner. They scolded their teacher and made him/her cry. They touched their female teacher's face or body improperly, and that it is today's typical sexual harassment.

In the same battlefield, the school organized war drills. Lessons went on halfway, the alarm sounded, and the schoolteachers and students were supposed to run out of the school building as soon as possible to the open ground to assemble, and the assembly is this battlefield. It was a failed military exercise. 800 teachers and students packed in the hallway and the staircase at both ends of the hallway. There was nowhere to rush away, and people began to pile up on the fallen ones. The most unfortunate boy, Zeng Xing, was at the bottom. He was trampled under the feet of the crowd. I don't know how many people stepped on his body; his head was trampled, too. His eyeballs squeezed out of his eye sockets—horrible! We never did the war drill again.

Let's come back and continue to recall that group fight set up by Wang Jin and Gu Jin Zhu. Wang called a hitman. His name in Jianghu is WaZi. Gu called another hitman. He was high-profile in JiangHu. He was wearing a long white scarf and sunglasses with long hair. He used his mature voice and said to WaZi: "Do you still want to fight?" WaZi was speechless. He would rather lose this fight than break the rules and epics of the underworld. Within one minute, without a move, without any body contact or fist exchanges, the incident ended silently, and the winner stroked the mule's shoulder and exited.

We as observers were not satisfied. We wanted to see a fight and blood. We did see another bullying, a group of gangsters bullying Yang Tong, the only son of the Professor Yang Ze Qi in the mining faculty. They knocked his head with a piece of sharp rock. His blood sprang out high in the air. And we did see the same group of gangsters bullying Wei Yan Lin, a non–Steel Courtyard teenager. They knocked his head. His blood sprang out high in the air. Both Yang and Wei suffered brain disabilities from their injuries/stitches.

Gu, as the winner of the group fight, was never able to show up at our school again. The high school attached to the Steel Courtyard was always our school and not his, even though he won there twice, officially and underworldly.

Wang was the loser of the group fight but was able to come back to our school gloriously. He took part in the college/university entrance examination preparation courses. He sat in the first two rows as he had before, and as a student was very well taken care of by the head teacher, who had the power to arrange seats for all his/

her fifty-plus students in the class. He passed the college/university entrance examination with a high score, 340 in 1979, and Wang Jin could study at the Nankai University physics department in Tian Jin. He ranked number one in my class.

14

New Year's Celebration

The New Year's celebration is a great joy for the children. Fireworks are fun and not expensive, 0.21 yuan/100 pieces. We called them "small whips." When they explode they make a big crispy "bang," just like the *pia* the whipping makes. Making a hundred *pias* is easy: with a bamboo pole or wooden stick, set off the lower end of the ignition, and a hundred crisp explosions will make up the atmosphere, bringing happiness. The sound in the ear and a cloud of smoke cheer people up. This is a rich man's game. We poor boys had 1 yuan or 2 for the entire New Year's celebration only. We could not spend it within a minute. We prolonged these 100 fireworks by igniting them one by one, perhaps ten for today, another ten for tomorrow, and so on. We carefully portioned these 100 bundled fireworks into pieces. We made sure the wick was still in its original place. Fireworks or paper-wrapped fire powder in kids' hands is a kind of safety issue anywhere, right? We were allowed, but only during the New Year's celebration time and no other. We took a one- or two-foot-long cotton line to serve as a wick. It could keep the cotton ignited for a long time and is longer than a match. Ignite the firework, place it somewhere on the wick, and then run away, plug the ears, and it pops an explosion. Courageous children like myself have always held the firework in our right hands, finger and thumb tip pinching the ends of the firework. What is the reason? The ignited wick burns so fast it will immediately detonate firecrackers, and it is too late to throw the firecrackers out of your hand in the explosion, and it will blow up in your hand, shock your ears, and you become stupid because of everyone's laughter. And pinching both ends of the firework can block the fuse burning all the way into the fire-powder body. If I had to cease fire, I just pinched it firmly. A firework blows up only when it leaves my hand. Happy end.

15

Repair of Pens

The repair industry is an all-encompassing place. It can be said that where someone has anything, there is a repair industry. When I was young, I had never seen oral orthopedics, spinal orthopedics, shape cosmetics, etc. Other than that, almost everyone has seen it.

Repair of pens. There was a crosstalk by Hou Baolin, who was a Chinese Mandarin language master, that teased them about repairing their pens. It said to see a person walking toward you. His pocket has only one pen; this is for sure a student. If there are two pens in his pocket, he is a teacher. If there are three pens in his pocket, he is a pen-repair guy.

Man named pen after the material used in its nibs. He has a steel sheet with a pen called a steel pen, and the gold one is directly called a gold pen. The material of the nib determines the value of the pen. The English Parker pen is the most famous. It is more a gift than a writing tool. In 2003 I went to Oxford University in England and shopped around the stationery store there, and I found that the long-unavailable Parker pens were still on shelves for a good price: 150 Pounds each. That's shopping around. I dared not buy it. Not because there were not enough funds in my pocket, but because I was afraid that when it broke there would be no place to repair it. The pen-repairing industry has disappeared in the last twenty years.

Accompanying the pen repair shop is the watch repair shop. Enter the door, and generally there will only be one master; that is, he is covering the repair bench and management/customer service, he is fully responsible for the work, paperwork, shipping and receiving work, collecting money and exchanging goods, writing carbonized copy documents, and the most important part, his repair skills. On one of his eyes he wears a magnifying glass, and he looks like an icon to his watch/clock repair industry. On the table are delicate watch-repair tools—tweezers, cones, pliers, small pliers, and a small iron container of kerosene. The kerosene is used to wash the mechanical core of the watch. With mechanical clocks (there were no electronic clocks/watches available at that time), after a long time of *tick-tock* you have to send the clock/watch to a repair booth, or an independent repair shop to remove oily sludge and wash it with kerosene, remove the sludge, add high-grade lubricants, and cover the back of the clock lid to finish. Good guy, five bucks a piece! The master, by the way, adjusts the spring-limit strap valve in the watch core so that it is accurate when it *tick-tocks*. How can you tell if your clock/watch is not working punctually? It's a radio station thing. Every hour the station plays a set of signals, demonstrating the timing: "Doodle-Doodle-Doodle-Doodle-Dee!" Then the male or female announcer reports: "The last note was XX o'clock, Beijing time."

The next one is the eyeglass shop or optics. They are the corrective devices for human beings to wear. Many people have congenital myopia or farsighted eyes. This is an eye disease that must be treated. But during the Cultural Revolution so many people suffered from it, but they left it as it was. They didn't want to wear glasses to correct their sight or to cover their weakness. Why was that? At that time, people had a concept that wearing glasses meant you read more. And reading more meant you were richer of knowledge. Finally, your rich knowledge would kill you, because Mao did not like you as an intellectual. It is said in a children's rhyme: "1, 2, 3, 4, 5, 6, 7, wearing glasses no future." I was surprised to find out that this discrimination is worldwide: "little four-eyes" is a derogatory nickname. Only one middle school classmate of mine, Xu Li, was awarded this "honour." Nobody expected that he would be able to study at a military school/university, and after his graduation, he became an officer. He wore glasses all his life. He was responsible for commanding the S-6 missile driven by vacuum electronic tubes, defending the sky of Beijing, the capital of the great motherland from 1983–1990, and is now a model of "coming from behind."

Decades had passed, and when we were at a reunion party, someone could not recall his name and surname, but called him by his nickname, "little four eyes," to identify him. This discriminate had once and for all been improved by 1975, when Deng Xiaoping substituted for the seriously sick Premier Zhou Enlai to preside over the work of the central government. He should start from grasping education—the ministry of education had a top intellectual Zhou Rong Xin as the educational minister.

It changed the entire atmosphere of school on all levels. We should take the opportunity and learn something from our textbooks, not from the plant workers, not from the farmland peasants, not from the military soldiers and so on. I took this chance to have my first-ever pair of glasses in my life, to correct the nearsighted condition my parents passed to me—they both wore nearsighted-corrective eyeglasses.

Deng did not have time to fire Mao's ex-girlfriend, the Tsinghua University revolutionary committee chief, Xie Jingyi, and assigned Liu Bing as the dean, then his reform try-out collapsed. Deng stepped down and left me alone with my pair of glasses in the middle of nowhere. The political atmosphere was tied again. I was about to set up a negative model as an "white pro," which is a politically blind textbook geek. My political standing ground was wrong. The members of my class committee decided that they would criticize me at the coming class political study period. Because I was not a class cadre, nor was I a regiment cadre, I did not have the right to participate in this joint meeting. I was just the leader of the fourth group of nine students, including me. And I was the English-language course representative. No one was willing to take the foreign language course representative role. I proudly and secretly call my fourth group the "Four Wild." In Chinese civil war history in 1947–1949, Four Wild was led by Lin Biao. It was the major military armed force to kick out the formal army, the National Army, all the way from mainland China to Taiwan. Lin Biao's Four Wild has yet to recover its reputation. In the class, my "Four Wild" was a group of bad reputation, poor performance. In our whole class during rural labour times, three groups of girls—1, 3, and 5—had too much food. The girls would pass it on to the all-boys groups, 2 and 6. My group 4 got nothing. As a group leader I had to find a way to get food, and that way was from fields. I sat in my "headquarter", which was my straw matrass "bed" on the muddy ground, sent a few boys to the left to go with the flow to get cooked canteen food, and sent a few others a moment later to the right, to go to the fruit tree garden to pick some yet-to-mature fruits to satisfy our hungry. That was not a perfect idea. The yet-to-mature fruits made us feel hungrier. Anything went wrongly I should confesse to the temp teacher Wang Xue and reviewed it. My Four Wild had a bullying talent number one in the Steel Courtyard, the invincible Luo Jianguo, his father was the defense section leader in our courtyard. He had guns. This was the kind of person who could bring a gun to work. Luo Jianguo was therefore the number-one buster in the whole class. He pretended to have a sore throat, trying to get medical tablets served by the medical and health staff attendant, Ms. Wang Shuling. She was also my classmate. He was trying to get a few mint-and-sugar pills, delicious in the time without sugar. His trick was no good. Wang Shuling was wiser, and she detected that the "itching throat" was not red nor thick, which it was supposed to be. The bad boy must be punished. He was chasing her, that's all. She opened her apricot eyes widely and gave Luo an injection. "No problem. You will be fixed," said Wang to her "patient." There was no medicine in the shot at all, distilled water only. He deserved a prick and pain! Presumably that was the only time she had practiced medicine in her life. The effect was good. From then on Luo Jianguo did not chase female classmates in his own class but turned to a girl one grade below us. That grade was called the "wearing-a-hat class," because the elementary school switched to a five-year graduate system in that year, when we were in Grade 6 and they were in Grade 5. We all graduated in the same year. My Four Wild team member had talented boys as follows:

A Beijing subway chief designer Cheng Xinping. He failed two exams out of three. The nickname was "Big West" when he finally entered the Northern Transportation University. His cheap daddy only rewarded him a bottle of soda for his three years of frustrated exams. And it was not even a Coca-Cola, nor a Pepsi. It was Arctic artificially coloured, artificially flavoured soda only, 0.15 yuan plus deposit each.

A rich man, Guo Guangming. He was the richest one in my class of fifty-four.

An unofficial table tennis champion in Beijing. In China any official table tennis champion can smash the rest of the world. And my Four Wilds team player Wang Xiao Dong smashed them all. I should mention myself as one of his table tennis practice partners. The other one was well known as the CEO of Kun Tai Group in Beijing. His name is Zhou Jian. Together we fixed him till he could challenge and beat the official champions.

Repair of the human body is practiced medicine; repair of the human brain is education and examination. The physical action of the human, sports-game technical and tactical repair is the coach. They are all generally in repair industries.

I should mention our cooking pot. It was a cast-aluminum cooking pot. The entry of aluminum metal into thousands of households happened shortly before the Cultural Revolution. It was first seen in the Korean War in 1950: the U.S. military's aluminum kettle. There was already less and less scrap metal from the recycling industry, and it was even rarer to use aluminum. Slowly, there was a domestic version of the cast-aluminum kettle. It was the same shape as the American version, and the British version is very different. Later, after 1980, I learned that the logistics of the U.S. military were very massive, its drinking water could be Coca-Cola, among other soft drinks. Marching to any battleground, they also do not bring their own kettles. Only twenty years ago I got to know that the Communist Army/Chinese People's Liberation Amy, or PLA in short, logistics are also strong: their drinking water can be Guizhou Maotai, a kind of 53 percent–65 percent alcohol containing the top spirit in China.

Corrupted army, broken party, do they deserve fixing? Time to de-power them now, the Red Axes.

Oct.2nd, 2019

中国式摔跤

中国式摔跤有许多种，不成门派就是最常见的，存在于儿童少年当中。他们不论闹着玩儿还是打架都涉及摔跤，各方抢先抓住对方衣服肩膀上的布，然后他们往自己怀里一拉，有招数的孩子在与此同时还用自己的脚绊之。对方下盘不稳，就会失去身体的重心，也就是向侧身倒下，把对方也拉倒，后面跟着系列碾压和翻滚，谁都不肯在下面认输。在上面呆着也不容易，随时有被掀翻，骑压的可能。往下搂，搂住对方腰的，也常被对方搂住头，于是双方角力开始，腰部力量是制胜的关键，再往下搂，抄到一条大腿就好了，对方单腿跳，随时可以被摔倒，同时其自身的重量会把对方带着一起摔倒，两人一起倒地之前，发生了一些可怕的招数，锁脖。把对方的头，夹在自己的左侧或者右侧的腋下，双手扣紧，往地上一坐，对方必然头朝下，屁股朝上翻倒，四肢再也发不出力来，蹬地面能使两人原地打圈圈，双方身体绞着，分不出胜负，但气势上，被锁脖的一方不占任何优势。高级一点的动作是过肩摔，不让对方缠住自己的身体，在对方扑上来的一瞬间，下腰，拿捏住对方身体的某个部位，使其腾空，然后双手向自己后方一撩，对方即从自己的肩膀上飞到后面去，嘴啃地了。据说这叫小搬。用这个对付不会摔跤的对方，百试不爽，而且不费力气。卖关子，卖破绽，给对方自己的后背，两人对峙时，尽量压低自己的上身，把后背亮给对方来抱，突然正起身，用后背扛起对方整个身体，对方必然头朝下，从你的后背上下滑到地面，两脚却在空中乱蹬，此时进可以反身压住对方，退可以向前进一步，甩掉对方，一走了之，任凭对方狗吃屎，或者脸朝地。大背胯，不实战，没有见到过一次，我的儿童时代，附近就是农村，农村到了收获季节，就叫我们去农村学农劳动，向贫下中农学习，一般性劳动就是捡麦穗，打场，抱麦子，这都与场院，这个活动地点有关，到了场院，到了一大堆粮食，或者一大堆麦秆秋秸的地方，我们就开始练摔跤，也从中获得了无穷的欢乐，同时学到了一些摔跤的基本技巧，有心眼儿的孩子，还受人调教，在此时此地，卖出几招来博大家一笑，像我这种每摔必倒，连摔连倒的笨孩，最后也可以学会摔跤，就是进入摔跤竞技体育的门槛，你要学摔跤，须先学会挨摔。身体的任何部位着地，都不会因此受伤，才叫做会挨摔。摔跤，你们去爱吧，我可是挨摔挨够了。

奉送童谣一个，娱乐至上：

吧唧吧唧吧，

摔个大马趴。

马趴没摔好，

摔折了腰。

请来了吧唧医生来看病。

打了吧唧针，

吃了吧唧药。

为什么三天不见效？

笑！笑！！笑！！！

念完了童谣，大家一起憋住不笑。谁先笑了谁输，输了就要认罚。赢了的孩子打输了的孩子的手心，边打边把上述的童谣再说一遍，带节奏，有轻重。

队式摔跤没听说过吧？不是打群架，而是"骑马作战"。一个小朋友当马，背着另一个小朋友赤手空拳去拉扯另一对这样的人。这是体能高消耗之战，往往马交一个回合，已经分出胜负。

骑驴也没有听说过吧？两队小朋友，由队长出石头剪刀布，负者当驴头，本方队员一个挨一个撅起屁股，头顶着前面小朋友的屁股当驴背。胜者由队长当先锋，几步助跑，跳在空中，分开两腿，骑到最接近驴头的对方的小朋友的后背上。后面胜者一个接一个地飞骑上驴们的后背。没有发生驴的体力不支倒地重来，队长就在驴背上跟驴头石头剪刀布地理论起来，直到决出下一轮哪方是驴，哪方骑驴。连续输几轮的驴头肯定被本方队员，也就是驴背们骂死或者揍死，然后换驴头，接着玩。这个骑驴游戏比竞技体操当中的跳马刺激多了。跳马使用的是器械，而骑驴，是我们的清瘦的小身体飞起来，砸的那个驴是真人，所以这个游戏又叫做"砸驴"。

打沙包是考验小孩子奔跑，急停，转身，躲闪，手眼身法步全面考验的身体协调性的游戏。孩子们不论男女都可以混队参赛。地上隔8米10米的划两条线，打包的队分站两条线外，而躲包接包的队全体在这两条线之间来回跑，出界或跨界算出局。一个是躲闪，被飞行的包击中者出局。一个是接包，空接一个飞翔的包可以挽回一条命，就是本方出局的一个队友可以回到场上继续奔跑躲闪或者接包参战。接不住包，掉地上了算被击中，要出局的。全队都被击中，再无续命者为输，则攻防转换。这个游戏象棒球，不过比棒球激烈多了。攻击方人人都是投手，捡包，递包给本方更有杀伤力的投手还体现了团队精神。而捡包递包时飞行的包被对方接到也不算。所以在捡包递包时，动手的这个孩子要高声吆喝"递包----！"以免起纠纷。而投手专门朝对方小朋友的下三路招呼，因为下肢接不到包，这种打法安全，可以尽早实现攻防转换。想象一下吧，中间十个孩子紧张地左右躲闪，来回奔跑，甚至对撞，摔倒，两条线外的攻击方的孩子们，一边五个，捡包的，递包的，投包的，虚晃一下的多么热闹？出局的孩子们往往是身体协调性稍差被包击中，或者体力不支倒地，被近距离砸中者。而担任捡包，递包者，则是攻击性不强，老给对手投好包，让人家接住续命者。

以上各项游戏都追求公平竞争。无器械的身体接触性的对抗就最讲究公平。

铁丝网也能做出玩具

那时候我们有什么? 我们什么都没有。这是一个不负责任的回答, 实际上, 我们还是有些什么的。我们有铁丝网, 有水塘, 夏天可以当游泳池, 冬天可以当溜冰场, 我们有刻刀。我比别的孩子们, 可能会用多一些工具, 比如说老虎钳子, 锤子, 锯条什么的, 还多了一个谁也不再玩的老古董, 就是计算尺。拉计算尺, 进行指数对数运算, 是我从小就会玩儿的事情, 算什么呢, 算利率? 不对, 算的是驴打滚儿的阎王债, "白毛女"里面的杨白劳, 他为什么白劳作了一辈子? 最后还得把女儿喜儿搭进去给债主黄世仁家作女佣还债, 就是因为他不会算这个债务的利率。其实黄世仁也不会算, 而是他的账房或者管家穆仁智会。我会算也没用, 到头来, 女儿出嫁, 进了黄家的门, 还不是黄世仁的黄? ! 说点别的吧, 我有一把老虎钳, 又叫克丝钳, 平嘴钳, 它可以把8号铁丝剪断, 但是我是一个八岁的儿童, 手没有那么大的握力, 往往只能在铁丝上划一道痕, 然后掰来掰去，直到铁丝脆断，其断口是不规则的石块茬口，根本没有什么晶粒，晶变，晶层断裂处的科学具象。剪断这一段铁丝网，我把它连偷带拿地带回家，然后把它上面的铁刺，铁蒺藜一个一个的剥下来，钳子改锥榔头一起上，10号铁丝做的铁刺稍微软，但是太短，发力不好，就会从钳子口滑脱，然后就是几滴鲜血和呲牙咧嘴的疼痛，手上又添了一道疤痕。到了招募空军，听说还有可以上航天器，当宇航员的机会的时候，这些手上的伤口，使我去报名的勇气都没有，因为据说飞行员的身上不能有疮疤，反过来说，就是有了疮疤就当不了飞行员，体检不合格。话说回来，去找铁刺的铁丝网，是弯的，如何把它弄直了也是一门技术，有人用锤子，我喜欢用钳子，钳子能把铁丝弯弯，就能把它弄直。钳子慢慢扳直的铁丝，不带或者少带应力应变，其金相组织尽量少有变化，金相组织无变化，铁丝就没有局部软，局部硬的情况出现。这些知识是怎么获得的，实践出真知，你去扳几根铁丝以后，也会无师自通，都不要人点拨。弄完了，还不懂的，可能不容易在金属加工业混。好了，材料准备好，做个什么玩具呢，冷兵器吧，弹弓，弹弓枪，热兵器吧，火柴枪，砸炮枪，这些个男孩人手一把的东西，我都做过，弹弓是最简单的。材料就要求大，牛皮筋，听诊器的软管，橡皮条，都是好东西，还要一块真牛皮做弹兜。做好了弹弓，给小朋友当中的射击高手，他能够一弹射下在树上叫个不停的蝉。打个麻雀什么的，不在话下，一般都是弹无虚发。水浒当中的没羽箭飞石打英雄，其实也没有什么惊人的本领，但是我们小时候，他张清就是我们心中的偶像。

器械相斗，有些不公平。人用弹弓打鸟，对鸟来说不公平。人用铁丝网圈人，圈牲口，圈地，这也不够公平。

3
证章

　　证章，文革刚开始时，校办工厂就开始了疯狂的，主席像章制作。精致的铝片上，漆毛主席头像的像章，人手一枚。人手一枚在中国是个什么概念？发行量，据保守的估计，也与人民币硬币的发行量不相上下，你们回顾一下文革初期，身无分文的穷鬼有的是，但是身上胸前没有佩戴毛主席像章的人却不好找。因为中国是人口大国，文革开始时也有7亿人，几亿枚证章，在不过一年的时间里，几乎免费地流向全中国乃至全世界。证章制作作坊及工匠，一下成为抢手货，时装，时髦，都没有它流行。标准的或者是理想的证章搭配，是胸前左侧上别一枚五星形毛主席像章，下面别一枚长方形为人民服务证章。两枚刚好，多了炫耀，少了遗憾。五角星行证章难寻，因为军事副统帅林彪就戴这个，而五角星在中国就是军方的符号。也可以用椭圆形章代替，长方形的为人民服务证章一定要原件，因为周恩来总理就佩戴这

个，白底，红字，金边，红字是怎么涂上去的呢，用一根
医用注射器针筒，来抽取一针筒的红漆，带上针头，用
手工，巧妙地注射到模块上的金属沟槽里面，然后去
烤箱里，用红外光线烘干，出来的效果堪比景泰蓝，至
于它为什么没有形成景泰蓝工艺？那个时候谁负责工
艺，技术？都醉心于无限忠于毛主席，但是一个共同
的特点是，制作完成的毛主席像章，发放到个人手里
之后，绝对没有再加工后期制作改造的份，人们对他忠
诚的程度是无以复加的，也许是稍加改动，即有沦为现
行反革命罪犯的嫌疑，多一事不如少一事。人们很快就
转变其动手能力和创作能力，转去攒沙发，制作木头家
具去了。结婚领证前后，才能获得买一个大衣柜的许可
票据，这还不代表你一定能买到，买到也不代表你一
定能运回家，一个三合板，好一点的五合板拼成的，双
门或三开门大衣柜，通常由一辆人力三轮平板车拉回
家。我，为了以后能娶上媳妇儿，还特地学会了蹬三轮
儿，一根棉绒绳，一块棉被或者毛毯，下面铺着上面捆
着，三轮后面一般是媳妇骑着车跟着，你看她单手扶
把，另一只手在大衣柜上助推一路，意得志满地犹如
押送替她背负战利品的俘虏。上海的插队回城知青，
或者根本就是放弃插队而返回城市的年轻人，更是手
巧，有个男孩，居然用家里及邻里每月限量的柴禾票，
买来劈柴，一根一根的拼装成地板，在新房里铺上的

全部实木地板，这心气和这手艺，迷倒多少人家小妹。什么电器化了？台灯自己制作，日光灯自己制作，收音机自己制作，电视机自己制作，买不起电视机上那个显像管，降格以求，制作一个电视伴音，可以收听电视台的节目，调频收音机的鼻祖了吧，因为当时连调频广播的电台都没有，调频收音机是在80年代以后，才有用处的东西。我自己于1980年才拆了我的木头单人床（因为我有大学生集体宿舍的一个床位啦），用木板，自制分频器，购买高频头和当时最先进的橡皮边包纸盆大口径低音喇叭，制作了一个音箱。第一是因为钱紧，做不起两个；第二是因为当时还没有立体声技术传入中国。电台，磁带，唱片什么的都是单声道。一两年后，我父亲从西德带回国一套家用高保真立体音响设备以及一些立体声唱片，包括贝一到贝九交响乐，卡拉扬指挥的。从此它变成了我的泡妞利器，我给它剪裁缝纫了一个盖头加披肩，上面是白丝绸，周边是镶金丝红色摩力克装饰专用的布料，使它象一座阿拉伯王子的雕像。不过阿拉伯世界的清真教义不许他们塑立人物或者神的像。据我母亲说，我爸从西德弄回来的这套高级玩意儿的音质其实还不如我自己制作的那个音箱呢。母爱如海啊。

暗房技术，现在的男孩们无一人可以掌握，但当时我们十岁一过就会了，直到8964，此方大涨，成为攻破中共当时谎言的利刃。

印刷电路板的绘画和腐蚀，有点化工的味道。这个合我的胃口。我去北京城里的西四和西单北一带地方的二手电子器材店买回来一块上面有铜的电木板，五毛钱0.50/2寸见方，挺贵的哈。拿回家来，往铜板上画油漆电路图，把油漆下面的铜板遮住，使这部分铜不接触腐蚀铜的三氯化铁溶液。这个三氯化铁上哪儿弄去呢？化学老师家里的熊孩子，也就是我在这方面比较灵，当时就知道三氯化铁是水泥快干剂，战备工地上就会有，钢院的丁家大院里，那一坛子一坛子里装的黄绿色液体就是那玩意。我偷了一个家里的瓷碗，（不能用金属容器装腐蚀金属的液体，这个我也懂哈）盛了半碗端回家，泡上画好漆的电路板，放到煤炉上煮起来了。没有用油漆包住的铜板渐渐腐化，消失，溶液变黑变深绿并且发兰。我成功了。碗底结了黑色物质，不能再用来吃饭了。我就假装失手打破它，挨了几句骂。用这块自制的印刷电路板，我制作了一个单管收音机。用这部晶体管收音机，我跟着北京广播电台的英语广播讲座学了好几年的英语。为了证明它是我亲手制作的，下面特别列出零件清单及其价钱：

磁棒0.30元/6厘米

漆包铜线圈, 自制, 不要钱

单联可变电容器, 调台用, 1.05元

三极管0.10元/只, 单管机指的就是这个单独的, 起放大作用的晶体管

二极管0.5元/只, 要两个

几个电容电阻都很便宜, 不到0.07元/个

可变电阻0.20/个, 调音量用

耳机2.11元/个。因为单管机根本就带不动喇叭, 只能用耳机收听它放大了以后也不太响的声音。

耳机插孔0.78/个, 太贵了, 自己动手用罐头皮和电木垫圈做了一个。

到了1988年, 市面上还没有歌厅, 但是已经有了录像放映厅, 0.3-0.5元/位, 放映香港武打片, 日本电视连续剧什么的, 007系列尤其受广大观众的喜爱, 但是他们听不懂台词。听不懂没关系啊, 有我呢。我是大学没毕业就担任编外英语汉语口译员, 我一个翻译可以同时招呼4, 5个鬼子呢, 现在加上我借助单位的录像放送设备, 配上自制的麦克风, 充当放映员, 同声翻译加配音演员, 一会儿装女声, 一会儿装老头, 绰绰有余。一到晚上, 各地来京出差, 进修, 开会的煤矿工程师, 技术干部们就在我的住所里集合看外国录像, 我可以整夜干这个还乐此不疲。我的"辛勤"的劳动结下了意想不到的善果: 我去煤矿出差, 一旦碰到被我在北京用

放映外国录像招待过的人,这出差任务就会顺利加圆满完成,我不一定认得他们,但是他们都认识我,而且主动相认。这样工作起来根本就不用我费事,不需要潜规则,也不走后门。我好像很正派哈。我们在一起玩大的,叫做发小。这一层关系非同一般,是无价之宝。

至于我个人到底会些什么?或者制作成功过什么东西?可以在列在下面搏大家一笑,音箱,电视伴音,单管,中波调幅收音机,矿石收音机,耳机插座,电烙铁,冲洗黑白胶卷,洗照片,放大照片,至少用两种字体,写标语,条幅,等线体,仿宋体,隶书,用欧体写大字报楷书,单反机摄影,用摄像机拍摄录像,有录像机转录,下载电视台节目,翻译外国电视片,修自行车,修汽车,修船和造船,电焊,电工,水暖工,做中餐,作文,做范文,尤其擅长写信,中文英文俱佳,达到同辈人的上乘水平。骑自行车,骑三轮车,驾驶汽车,驾驶汽艇,驾驶铲车,驾驶升降台。至于做官?做生意?呵呵。

4
铲雪

铲雪, 是一件不计成本工时的事。1987年初, 在哈尔滨遇到大雪, 通勤车不能开了, 全城上至哈尔滨市委书记, 下至普通机关职员, 一起上街铲雪, 一小时后, 道路畅通, 全城的路就通了。下面, 就说一下什么叫通勤车? 大一点的单位有1到2辆大巴, 平时星期1-6, 每天早上6:30出发, 按规定路线, 规定的接人站停车, 开门, 接本单位员工去上班, 每天下午5点又出发, 再按规定路线, 规定的地方, 停车, 开门, 送本单位员工下班回家, 这是一种福利, 叫通勤车, 官拜局长, 副局长, 为了亲民, 也享受此福利, 不用专车接送。部长级干部, 不再用通勤车了, 有专职司机, 机关发司机的工资, 配专车, 机关出钱出指标买的车, 乘客一个子儿都不用掏, 就可以小汽车接来接去, 司机因故迟到了, 还得写检查, 在开会时念这个检讨。小汽车的级别, 直接标志用车人的级别, 国产上海牌六缸, 进口伏尔加, 合资的大众桑塔纳, 德国造奥迪，日本造丰田皇冠，日产蓝鸟等，单位车队的，好一点的车子，基本上是干这个的，我在的单位首长级别较高，达到了建国初期的八级，所以1960年代就配置了一辆奔驰220，那辆车的复色漆之厚重，车身之重，关车门都是砰的一声，震撼附近本来就胆小的群众。中国官员就会吓唬老百姓，因为他们有超越法治的权力，可以任意逮捕，羁押，拷打百姓，而不用走法律程序。他们的车子绝非今日法拉利，或者劳斯莱斯可以比拟的，因为在当时车子太少，一般人想买自行车票还得抓阄，还都抓不到，作弊花样百出。抓不到阄就买不了自行车，更甭说汽车和私家汽车了，统统没有，我第一次坐奔驰，还是到了奔驰家乡，德国的西德以后才坐上，德中友协会长海尔穆特。迪尔先生的太太，克里斯拓。迪尔夫人，亲自驾驶，关于她的故事，我有专门章节介绍，我们是父子二人坐在后排，俨然贵宾了一把，数十年后，当我开着自家的奔驰，君临天下的感觉，不再附体。是因为车多了，还是因为90年代奔驰引进了一个克莱斯勒合作伙伴，把自己贵重的零件，换成轻薄的那种，关门时不再发出砰一声，而是噗的另一种声音，连奔驰标识性的喇叭双重声，也卖给了丰田，自己却留下了通用的单音。中国民歌唱法男高音李双江变成了电视台演小丑的潘长江，金嗓子变了。这仅仅是一个例子。

还是回来说铲雪吧，我小的时候，北京城里的雪可大了，下完雪，我的小哥把我拉到北海公园去打雪仗，从山顶打到山涧，滚了一身雪。雪深到可以没顶，把我全身湿透的那种，我作为一个六岁的小屁孩儿，半身埋在雪里，顽强抵抗，比我大个七八岁的，小表哥，他猖狂进攻，我狼狈防守，两个人都高兴坏了。空气太新鲜了，那时候根本就没有空气质量差之说。

1984年春天，我和中国矿业学院北京研究生部的同学们，在北京西郊颐和园的昆明湖冰面上，打了最后一次雪仗。

1995年，我开上了铲雪车。那是我作为新移民到加拿大后做的第一份工作。我的老板是赵俊，他当时是一名在多伦多大学就读的留学生。他给我发的工资是每个月800加元。而市政府雇佣的铲雪车手的工资是每小时40加元。这也就是说，他们干两天工作赚的钱，要我这个新移民干整整一个月。不论白天黑夜，不管周末还是假日，只要下雪，我就得出车户外铲雪。1995圣诞夜多伦多下雪了。这是我永远的记忆。

2012/2013年我又开上了铲雪车。这次是给我在加拿大安大略省士嘉堡开的波斯猫羽毛球馆的车道和停车场铲雪。给房东铲雪，他的物业管理员给我4500加元/月。老天保佑，我及时地停了下来。我的房东，越南人杰克张把他的领地用不到半价，也就是2000加元/月，包给了一位专业园艺及铲雪服务生。这个可怜的老头，他干了一个月就不行了。那一年的雪太大。房东杰克张不得不花1000加元/小时请来重装备公司，开着推土机，翻斗车，把停车场的雪堆起了好几堆，每个都有三层楼高。这些雪直到次年6月份才彻底化干净。

现在还在玩雪的孩子们，他们都是去滑雪场，先玩大回转，再玩小回转，高山降陡坡等滑雪项目，戴一副防雪盲的墨镜，还有偏光镜功能，这得要多少钱？我小的时候根本就没听说过。加拿大的安大略省有一处世界级驰名滑雪场，叫蓝山。在那里，我的独生女儿克里斯拓学会了初级滑雪。注意到了没有？我女儿与德国汤若望德中友协会长的太太的名字相同。

好了，回来铲雪吧，从房顶上，中国烧煤烧柴的烟囱里滴出的冷凝水，融化雪水，沿着老房子的屋檐，流了一地，随漏随结冰。就形成了一个一个的小斜山坡，这是冰道啊。踩上去必然滑倒摔跤，我们孩子们的家务事之一，就是铲除这一个一个的冰坡道。零下十几20度的冬天，那时候北京真有这么冷，一刀下去或者一镐下去，或者一锹下去，最多在冰面上多出一道冰白痕，剁不透，所以要一下一下的剁过去，直到全部冰被剁开，露出庭院地上的方砖表面，当时也没听说过谁家撒上一把盐，就能防滑不结冰的，撒盐太豪华了吧？屋里是一个烧煤的炉子，冬天从来不灭，炉膛外围是铁丝网，或者铁皮网，因为炉子外面很近的地方就是床铺，被子一旦近火就烧着火了。防护铁丝网或者铁皮网，上面搭满了洗过的袜子，被脚汗湿透的鞋垫儿，以及贴身的衣服，是内衣吗？不是，就是一种贴身小褂子，两肋开气儿的小背心，省布料嘛，夏天可以直接穿着出门的那种。衣服的复杂性，和进化到加拿大鹅的历史进程，以后另有篇章。这里防湿防冷，烘干鞋子袜子鞋垫什么的要紧，鞋子为什么是湿的？冬天的脚为什么会出汗？湿了的袜子，鞋垫和鞋子，要趁夜间脱下来烤干，那种布面布底的鞋子。哪里是什么普拉达，耐克和阿迪达斯？那些东西都是时髦，名牌。我们就是黑色灯芯绒面，里面塞棉花，布和浆糊及小线千层底，千针万线纳出来的鞋底。好看的是白色的塑料底，或者车轮胎的材料做的底。这是一种布棉鞋，有鞋带的还比较高级，无系带的叫豆包鞋，老头们穿着还可以，孩子们穿豆包鞋可是要被人家耻笑的，而买不起，自制的往往就是豆包鞋，裤子脚一定要塞进袜子里，不然冰雪倒灌进来，那个冷啊。我家的所谓富有，也就是有换洗的袜子，有时还穿得起尼龙袜子，而尼龙袜子不透气，弄得脚比较臭。但是它色彩斑斓，又时髦，还有松紧，所以臭就臭吧，臭美，这是当时流行的词儿呢，更富有的人家有毛袜子，就是在布袜子或者尼龙袜子外面，再套上一层，手工织就的毛线袜子。尤其是羊毛线织就的毛袜子，那才暖和呢，我只有过一双，还不懂得爱惜，穿着它去踢球，踢冰嘎儿，最后脚趾头露了出来，也就不能穿了，晚上一脱鞋，毛袜子全在脚心一带地方，孤处着呢，脚趾头冻的发痒，脚后跟上面的跟腱部分，是一溜粗糙的皮肤，给冻春了，冻裂了，弄不好就流血了。现在的孩子们有过如此苦难的经历吗？当时的我们，不论贵贱，不论大小，全都这德行了。我的被窝里有一个东西，是一把精致的铜壶，叫汤婆子，其橡皮制代用品又叫暖水袋。每天寒夜里，脚冰凉，又想挨上去取暖，又怕被烫着，奶奶在铜壶外面，包了一个布袋，我不会再被烫到了，那种现在叫做酸爽的感觉你有过吗？不是每个孩子都有的，我奶奶有好几个孙子外孙子。我是她唯一的宠物，也许是因为我是她的大孙子吧。小儿子，大孙子，老太太的命根子。比我大的堂哥表哥们就都没有，他们每天晚上怎么熬夜？睡前怎么处理洗脚水？我从来不想，室内没有下水道，当然也没有厕所，所以每天早晨洗漱，晚上洗脸洗脚，冷水还是热水？我真的都不知道！我反正是被大人用一条热毛巾，擦满香皂在我的脸上擦洗，反复擦洗。周末一到，或者两个周末才来一次的爸爸，带着我这个已经臭不可闻的小家伙，去公共浴室，或者叫澡堂子的地方泡澡堂子，现在都叫非常时髦的水疗馆了，去一次得花几百上千吧。我们当时洗一次两毛六哎，已经算好贵的了，因为别的地方当时也就是一毛两毛的，没有泡澡池，只有淋浴的地方，才五分呢。我爸带我去的澡堂子可是北京有名的华清池，王府井对面，从我奶奶家到那里是走路的距离，大家脱光了衣服，存进自己有钥匙的，带号码的床头柜里，这两毛六，包这个柜子，加一个铺有大白毛巾的大床吧，还包热的洗澡水呢，毛巾是蒸过的，连干毛巾，都是热的，洗浴不同阶段无限制地取用。进去泡澡去，三个温度的大池子，每个池子都能容下20人同时泡。泡到浑身泥壳变软，一搓就下来，出来自己搓，或者由爸爸代替搓，我是鬼哭狼嚎的，一是因为我太脏，二是因为爸爸的手太狠。反正不能用搓澡工了，搓澡工来了，那是要加钱的。另外我从小就听说，搓澡工原来都是太监，他们专门揪小男孩的小鸡鸡，他们的小鸡鸡就是小时候被人揪掉的，叫"扽了"。所以我是又怕又没钱，坚决不能找他们给我的后背搓澡。后来再跟表哥一起去东四一带的澡堂子，都形成不了这些记忆，为什么呢，是待遇变差了，还是服务变差？无从谈起，我和表哥张维清要互相搓背，仅此还有一些记忆，别的什么都忘得差不多了。2016年到上海，和穆军同学又体验了一把，几乎都没有感觉了，回到北京，和魏有志同学，又体验了一把，甚至和几名女同学一起又去北京小汤山的豪华浴场体验了一把，都没有那种我刚刚叙述出来的感觉了。人啊人，即苦即乐，极苦极乐，不苦不乐。这都是怎么了？到了东京，和王小东同学，去体验了一把日式洗浴，到了江苏溧阳，和全班同学一起去体验了一把露天温泉洗浴，到了法兰克福，体验了许多次罗马式的裸男裸女露天混浴。能不能说，我就是洪福齐天了呢？有，就是我这个人还没有彻头彻尾的腐化堕落，没有，会被喷死，对吧？陕西西安附近临潼的华清池，咱们也去过。 跟我新婚媳妇骆辑在那里度蜜月。泡得正高兴的时候，我被我所在的单位紧急召回————美国能源署的长官约翰.贺伯斯特先生在中国呢。他不满意配给他的翻译刘小明，想要我去当翻译。我呢，在他1985首访，1986年次访华的时候给他作过全程翻译。回来继续泡澡。荷兰的格兰德大酒店，那里的浴场咱们也去过，加拿大安省蓝山滑雪度假村的户外浴，咱们也去过，你能点出来的地方和点不出来的地方，咱们都去光着屁股遛过。2003年， 我和我的欧洲忘年交老朋友，荷兰人老包听说莱茵河水治理见成效，民众可以下去游水了。于是我们在德国河段顺着河堤的坡滑下水，嬉水如孩童。穿过至少五个欧洲国家的浪漫的莱茵河里露天洗澡搓泥一回。爽。2011年，我的大学全班同学在北戴河聚会。大家到了海滨浴场却不下去泡。我和好哥们儿加同班同学李小坡脱衣入水。当时还下着蒙蒙细雨。李在20-30岁时是健美运动员，现在50岁了，身材仍然保持得很好，腹部6块肌肉都还在，后背倒三角肌肉群形状如前。我呢，又高又瘦，两腿如鲁迅笔下的苦命祥林嫂，是圆规的两根脚，现在倒好了，叫大长腿。我的上身是溜肩膀加驼背，不好看。我的两条胳膊倒是像北美男孩一般粗壮有力还挺长。加在一起也不怎么样。这次我就给他李小坡当回托儿吧。再说多点，就是吹牛了吧？1995年，我刚到加拿大的时候找不到工作，就去给我们的偶像周润发跑龙套。我还当了一回发哥的替身呢，裸替，拍的就是洗浴的戏。拍完了戏，就到了晚饭时刻。发哥厚道地给我们跑龙套的小哥们儿加餐，每人一份，半只大龙虾！可以不就烙饼就吃得饱的那么大的龙虾。我们当然更爱他了。

　　本章以铲雪开头，以洗浴收尾。没毛病吧？这是一种什么生活方式？什么行为方式？什么思维方式？大家琢磨去吧。

5
菜刀

　　菜刀，算冷兵器还是厨具，我没法界定。共和国的十大元帅之前几名，贺龙元帅在年轻时用菜刀造反起家，他用菜刀砍谁呢？砍盐商。贩盐的商人有盐，也就有钱。在1920年及以前，中国内地盐是贵的，不可多得的，属于政府管控物资，就像烟和酒一样，是政府专营专卖品，贺龙凭两把菜刀当了劫匪，杀盐贩子，弄到盐，再换成钱。用钱就可以把冷兵器菜刀换成热兵器枪了。有枪就当上了大土匪。后来他接受了共产党的"领导他们劫匪的核心力量是1921才成立的中国共产党，指导他们犯法的思想理论基础是1848就形成的马克思列宁主义。"这可是毛泽东的原话。由匪而兵，由兵而官。中共在1949全国除台湾金门马祖外取得了政权以后不久，大家评比，谁拥兵多，又没被敌手打死，也没被自己人整死的，就数他贺龙了。于是仅有的十大元帅中，他坐了前几名元帅的交椅。这个故事对任何一个男孩来说，都是励志篇之首。我第一次亲眼见识到用菜刀闹革命，正好是六岁，在我家。1966年文革爆发，大学，中学和小学的红卫兵，红小兵们到处非法抓捕他们的老师，领导，甚至是同学。有一天晚上，来了一伙人，到我家，7栋309的邻居310去抓本大学图书馆的馆长陈放先生。当时他的北京钢铁工业学院图书馆在北京的藏书量排名第四。前三名有北京图书馆，北京大学图书馆和北京师范大学图书馆。陈放一家四口住三居室的独门单元房里。叫门他不开，暴力敲门他更不开门了。这一伙人可都是大学生或者大学毕业生，他们当中的匪徒性格丝毫没有随着读书比别人多而少了或者没了。他们没有回去请示领导，拿个什么入户搜查令，逮捕证什么的再来实施抓捕陈放先生，而是马上转过身来叫我家309的门。我们已经被那种暴力敲门声吓坏了，就哆哆嗦嗦地开了自家的门。他们要问我们借一把菜刀。我家只有一把菜刀，就毫无保留地借给了他们。现在看来叫做授之以柄，把刀把子交了出去，自己任由他们宰割。这是大家在讨论的所谓奴性吧。当时我不懂。他们当中一个最想表现革命的"小将"挥刀砍了又砍310的门，直到门被砍破，砍开，陈放先生其人被这伙人当着自己老婆的面，当着自己两个儿子的面，一个16岁，另一个才14岁，连揪带打的提出310，活擒下了三层楼梯，抓捕而去。菜刀砍豁了刃，还给了我家，我们一声怨言都没有，不敢。陈放先生的俩儿子，叫大肥和二肥，都比我大，此后不知所踪，听说插队去了。不久他家被迫腾出三间房当中的两间，给一对后勤人员夫妇带仁儿子的家庭了。陈放先生在全院师生员工参加的批斗大会上被押上主席台，一边接受批判，发言带口号式的点名批判，一边被"坐土飞机"，脸上涂鸦，脖子上挂写有自己名字，名子上还打上红色叉子，和欲加之罪名的牌子，屈辱式的身体，姿势迫害。羞愤的一介书生陈放先生之后自杀了。个人的尊严都没有了，活着干嘛？谈何人权？！对了，当时还没有"人权"这个词儿呢，至少是这个词儿在中国还没有，在中国共产党内提出人权思想的人叫陈独秀（1879-1942）。他和他的思想都早早被干掉了。直到1978年，中国共产党统治下的中国才略微提到人权。此后又把人权和吃饭对立起来，弄得一塌糊涂。最近又听我的从小学到大学的同学马昆松说，陈放先生自杀并没有身亡，1977年他在同一间房子里，7栋，还见过他。而他的大儿子大肥的大名叫陈兆志，在钢院作了教授，用轧钢机械原理轧制方便面条。2019年7月29日，陈教授在北京八宝山革命公墓被捕，罪名是他在中国官方给李鹏举办的火化仪式上高呼口号，"打倒李鹏！""8964刽子手血债血偿！"我现在是在中国以外，有言论和写作的自由，可以回忆并且笔录一些史实。我不写这些文字，你不读这些文字，或许这段历史就永远被尘封了。文革到底有多么可怕，没有什么事件能这么长时间地，这么广泛地涉及各种人物，包括举菜刀的和挨刀的，这么深重地残害人，残害物，残害事。到底是怎么回事，不是一句话，一篇文，一本书或者一个博物馆能够弄清楚的。

过了一年多，轮到了我父亲。他没有从家里被抓捕，而是从他上班的理化系办公室直接抓进了一间窗户钉了木板的学生宿舍，12斋。使他倒霉的文革大运动里面的分运动叫做清理阶级队伍。我父亲将要被菜刀们清理出革命阶级的队伍，加上一个似是而非的罪名：国民党特务嫌疑。这可是最要命的罪过了。1911年，国民党（1919-今）先于共产党（1921-今），在孙中山的领导下革了封建王朝清廷的命，后来国民党跟共产党结了死仇。这种仇恨不是西方政党之权斗，而是双方各自佣兵武斗，以战胜者屠尽战败者的古代战争方式夺权。1949-1966共产党反复清洗国民党在大陆的残余。好了，现在身边出了个国民党，还是特嫌，那还得了？整！往死里整！！文革结束以后，我父亲的中学同班同学聚会时，大家不约而同地发现，他们全是因为这个"特嫌"罪名挨了整，倒了霉。其源头是一位同学是国民党青年组织三青团的，他在文革时被揭发出来，是国民党三青团的，就被抓起来，打，拷打，刑求，批斗。酷刑之下，他在实在挺不住了的时候，就把全班同学都抬了出去，就是跟打他斗他的菜刀们说，他把全班每一个同学都发展成为国民党了。于是他抬谁，谁就被其所在单位的菜刀们非法关起来打，打到挺不住时，就也去揭发别人。可是一个班就这么几个同学，大家都被揭发，每人也揭发别人，弄成死循环了。1948年北京被傅作义将军不经过武装抵抗就交给共产党了的时候，这个中学班没有一个同学超过18岁。

当天，我母亲沈凤韻只是从家里准备了一份牙具和换洗衣物，交给来人，托他转交给我父亲程述武。当时，我母亲怀上了我弟弟。我父亲被关在钢院校园内一个地方我们都知道，但是不许去探望，是12斋大学生宿舍里，几个月不许他回一趟隔着一个大操场的家。半夜里，菜刀们悄悄地摸进我家，在7栋309我家唯一的一间屋子里，对我母亲，一位上海复旦大学毕业赴京作钢院基础部化学教研室讲师，全校屈指可数的几位女教师之一进行夜间秘密审讯。我妈妈除了无声哭泣，死也不让菜刀们抄家。他们要找我父亲的日记。日记是个人隐私吧。直系亲属都不许偷偷互相翻看的。可是文革要消灭的就是这种个人尊严，个人隐私，个人财产及个人的一切。我和姐姐程婕都在睡觉，我却醒过来了，妈妈在抽泣，我则不敢出声，在被窝里发抖。我真是个没用的东西。我是当场唯一的男人，却不敢挺身而出，保护妇幼，而两位妇幼还正是我的亲妈和亲姐。那俩菜刀们简直就是畜生！他们夜入民宅，男主人不在家的民宅。他们也知道这个是作恶。居然也不声不响，不像以往那样，凡出场必高声宣读毛主席语录，呼喊革命口号，颐指气使。这些事使我母亲不能安心养胎，文革的冲击，深入到了我妈妈肚子里的我弟弟，这造成我弟弟程宣从生下来小心脏就患心律不齐。这些事都发生在一所当代技术文明大学的校园之内。本来身无寸铁的书生，一旦戴上一副红袖标，就可以举起一点也不文明的菜刀砍门，抓图书馆长陈放这样的文人；打我父亲程述武这样的大学物理化学教师，抓住他当时还有的头发，把他的头往铁架子床上撞，一次一次地撞击。这是要毁掉他的头脑。陈放馆长和我父亲他们具有比常人稍微富有一点知识的头脑，这才是毛不喜欢的。于是菜刀们就把他们打傻，以此来讨毛的欢喜。他们半夜趁我爸爸不在家，潜入我家欺负我妈妈沈凤韻这样的大学化学教师。　更变态的是，有个女版菜刀，她是钢院大学毕业生，留校当助教的王女士，姑且算作是一个准菜刀吧。她在非法关押审讯象我母亲一样从上海复旦大学毕业，赴京任钢院基础部化学教研室的男讲师罗泾源先生期间，动她还没有捏惯粉笔的小手去拔了罗叔叔胸膛上的，中国汉族男人罕有的胸毛！而且她是拔了一撮又一撮。也许罗叔叔胸膛上的体毛引起了菜刀们的猜疑，他掺有汉族以外的血统，而血统论是当时主宰一切的。"非我同族，其心必异"。是什么动机使菜刀们令那么多人陷入痛苦? 而且菜刀们狠, 准菜刀们更狠。北师大附中的女中学生就做下惨无人道的恶孽, 她把开水浇到了她所在中学的女校长的头上! 他们纷纷自觉自愿地当菜刀, 仅仅是因为文革以及之前之后的历次"革命", 都可以"杀人不偿命, 打人不违法, 抓人还立功", 还是人的从善本性到了菜刀们的身上就出现了变异?

菜刀们你们等着, 一个是中国效法西方真法制了, 法律当中不掺杂任何中国特色及变相修改。一个是只要你们还活着, 我程迅就一定会出头起诉你们, 送你们去法治监狱! 再一个就是你们死了以后, 在地狱或者类似的地方轮回到哪儿啦? 有没有转世回来人间的, 用你们自己的炼狱经历告诉后来的菜刀们及准菜刀们, 这样作孽永世不得超生? 没有。那就是说, 你们真的永世不得超生了。祝你们万劫不复!!

出了校园, 当时的情况更加不文明。我的爷爷奶奶住在北京城里的一座小四合院里, 无权无势。你们看看院子门口的两个石雕就知道了, 是狗, 不是狮子, 也不是麒麟等中国没有的高级虚构动物雕像。研究四合院门口石雕之后发现, 这个院子是给封建王朝的皇宫王府的卫士住的。石头狗给他把家里的大门, 他给皇上把紫禁城的大门。我爷爷从山东进京时是1920年间, 皇上早已于1905年退位, 那个卫士也跑了。他的家院子是空的，不知怎么就给我爷爷七大爷得到了。可能是我爷爷的姐夫有点权势，京汉铁路局的局长什么的吧，在北京怎么也得有几处房子吧。他的两个儿子王旭芹和王旭藻人人有自己的小院，我们叫东院西院的，连同我爷爷奶奶的院子，三处在一起，从同一个胡同口进去。文革一开始，也是那么一伙人冲进我爷爷的院子里来，宣布占领，抄家，没收，批斗。我才过六岁，家人赶紧把我领去西院。那里也不怎么样，前几天已经被抄过家了，高档家具无一幸存，全部被搬到不知什么地方去了。这次没有动菜刀，可能是因为我爷爷家已经衰败，家里没有什么古董字画了。他倒是一位开明之士，送自己的全部子女读洋和尚开的教会学校。男的上育英，女的上贝满，中学毕业都上清华，崇尚西学。我的奶奶七大娘在共产党1948进北京城之前就已经把自己的嫁妆变卖殆尽，支持家用及供子女上学。她自己也识字，会算术。这样的知识妇女在当时就是上过私塾，家里有钱的所谓大户人家。好了。红卫兵们没有抄到什么东西，就把我奶奶郭书箴和好奶奶张载之，姑姑程述舜和她的两个儿子，我的表哥萨本介，萨本仁，小名叫小不点儿及我大爷程述尧的儿子，我的堂哥程彭，小名叫灯灯（1980年代灯哥遵从母姓改姓改名为韦然。他的母亲是举国一流大明星上官云珠，文革时以自杀来证明自己清白，没有向菜刀们强加给她的"勾引毛主席"的罪名屈服认罪。菜刀们给她施用了最污浊的"刑罚",用肮脏的鞋底抽打她漂亮得令人窒息的脸颊。 参见韦然等著作"带雨云埋一半山"及"上海红颜旧事"。),和我程迅等7人赶出这座四合院,我们被赶出来的7人当中有6个没工作,没有收入,现在又无家可归,留下西屋的一小间给我爷爷,阿奶奶及他们唯一的孙女,我的大表妹程龚,小名叫琳琳等三人住,其他东南北三排好多间屋全部被菜刀们分给他们偏爱的菜刀们了。房子的主人,我的爷爷奶奶与这些"租客"并没有签租约,租客们也不交房租给房东,而是给没有房产的所谓"房管局",这种赤裸裸的抢劫通过象征性的房租就好像是合法化了,而那一点点房租少得可怜,都不够维修房屋的费用,甚至还没有水电费多。我记得有刘家五口,国家(姓国)五口,他们两家住北房。南屋,东屋以及门房住的那几家,不记得了。

"上帝给你关上了一扇门,必定为你打开另一扇窗"。天无绝人之路。我大姑程述舜在中央乐团做会计工作。这个乐团从北京市中心的东城区东华门,北京第一环城路之内的市中心,搬到了偏一些的东北方向上的朝阳区和平里,那里是北京第三环城路边。我姑姑分到了一个质量非常高的居民楼10区15号楼东单元的一个三居室单元房当中的两间。一间大屋朝南,老年妇女的挚爱,另一间小屋朝北,几个小伙子抗寒。要交房租,每个房间都有水暖暖器,厨房还有煤气, 加一个凉台,厕所还有坐式抽水马桶呢。70年代到八十年代末,这里变成了我们大家庭的聚会场所,平时我的仨表哥挤住在小北屋,我的两个奶奶和我大姑挤住在大南屋。过年,到了大年初一,全家老少二十多人就在这里席开两桌,大人们在南屋,小孩们在北屋聚餐。我是我奶奶的大孙子,所以她有一年亲自安排我坐了大人席。七十年代末期,我替我爸爸每个月去给奶奶送生活费25元。中国历来有这个传统,养儿防老,政府不管,政府更加不管跨朝代的遗老遗少。我祖母有好几个儿子,老大程述尧不是她生的,不管她的养老,还自己一身麻烦,他从文革以前就开始在上海被菜刀们欺负,祥见他的儿子,我的堂哥灯灯为他父亲写的专门著作"带雨云埋一半山"。大围女程述舜为她提供了三分之一间住房。老二程述铭过继给了无子女的好奶奶,他在文革中被菜刀们举报和整肃,说他对文革旗手,也就是毛的现任夫人江青表现不恭敬了。我的二大爷程述铭,他是一位杰出的天文物理学家,他在1960年代就首先提出用石英振荡为底,计量时空,是现在通行的石英钟它爸哈。位居中科院上海天文台的首席科学家的我的二大爷竟触电自杀!现在有一种说法,叫做被自杀,就是这种情况,菜刀们是杀人犯,但是他们能轻易逃脱法律的制裁。反正我的二大爷非正常亡故了,他是即管不了他的养母，我的好奶奶，也管不了他的生母，我的奶奶了。我奶奶生的二闺女程述岐过继给了好奶奶。她得管她的养母，我的好奶奶。于是能管到给我奶奶养老的，就只有我爸爸了。我奶奶的腿摔断，眼睛几乎失明，所以天天卧床，靠一部晶体管收音机，收听广播度日。我去了就躺在她身边报告我的考试成绩。物理100分，好；化学99.5分，遗缺了一个有机化合物命名的划线；数学100分，也好；三门主课棒就行了，哄得奶奶高兴。再晒晒副科成绩，英语95分，政治97分，全班第一，还评上了三好学生，不过奖状忘带了。每个班有50多名学生，每年就评2-3名三好生。1977年高考，我参加了，语文79分，数学67分，物理加化学66分，政治71分，总分283分，超过了北京录取分数线260分23分。不过我还是没有上大学。大学要给社会青年留位置，他们260分以上就可以上，我们是在校生，可上可不上，考过280分才给名额上大学。双标准哈。我的奶奶为此郁闷，离开了人间。这都是我的错。我直到1979年才考上大学。八十年代初期，我的小哥萨本仁在这里结婚生子萨龙。八十年代中期，我二姑程述岐的女儿，我的小表妹刘烨从山西霍县转学北京，在这处房子的厨房里完成高中课程暨高考补习，一举考入了邻近的北京联合大学。也是在这里，我的好奶奶对我进行恋爱暨婚姻指导，当时我对于娶一位教授的千金存有"攀高枝"的疑虑。好奶奶的一句话:"你爸爸也是教授。"一锤定音。还是在这里,我大姑姑对我进行毕业后工作方向指导,命令我毕业留校。我的表哥堂哥们则轮流指导我拉提琴,写大字,读书,读课外书和名著。对我们晚辈来说,这里是一片福地。而我们共同的长辈,祖辈三口,奶奶,好奶奶和大姑姑先后在这里辞世,她们再也没有回到那个不太吉祥平和的,挨过菜刀的四合院。

文革初期,被人用菜刀攻击民宅的,何止我上述的陈放馆长一个?我的大姨沈凤琴家在北京东郊的家也受到了这种野蛮攻击。暴力实施者诡称,他怀疑我大姨家的木板双人床的床头的夹层里可能藏有金条,于是他举起手里的菜刀就把床给劈开了。为什么要怀疑我大姨家藏金条?我大姨是上海迁京后在北京化工总厂任会计,我大姨父张善先是该厂的总工程师。她们在上海的化工厂被公私合营了。这些因素足够菜刀们找到借口了。我大姨家还因此失去了整个单元房,被逼迫搬到了当时是乡下的北京大学东墙外的一个小村里的一座四合院的东屋套间里。那里连自来水都没有,打井挑水,厕所也是公用的,全村仅有一个没有盖的公用水井,一处没有门的公共厕所。

用菜刀砍破民宅的门,进去绑架人,现在来算算,该当何罪?

手持武器

打家劫舍

绑架人质

刑讯逼迫，使受害人永久性残疾，头颅损害

变态折磨人，使受害者当众失去人的尊严

威胁人身安全，威胁受害人的亲属，子女的安全，霸凌她们

作案后擅离现场

并且伪造自杀现场

驱赶居民出住所

没收民宅

强占房屋

无约出租不属于自己的房产

这些罪行哪个不够坐几年牢的呀？可是在中国，到现在也没有人出来清算。文革后，我父亲从菜刀的利刃下苟活了下来，放生他的人，手中仍然握着菜刀柄，而有权拿刀的亦有权，甚至是同一个人，同一伙人。他们跟我父亲这样谈话：当初抓你是正确的。现在放你也是正确的。我的父亲居然无言地接受了这个"结论"。他已经经历了那么几年的"挂着"了。所谓挂着，就是不抓不放不判，你的问题就没有定性，不告诉你和公众是敌我关系还是人民内部矛盾，弄个"内定"来左右你。运动来了，风向对你不利时，拿你出来批判批判，羞辱羞辱，打压打压，整一整；运动过去了，风向稍微

缓解，就把你凉在一边，同时警告你，只许老老实实，不许乱说乱动。这个难受啊。上面说的所谓运动，不是健身活动那种体育运动，而是政治赶时髦那种运动。那么我们作为一介屁民，有没有资格举起菜刀呢？没有。包括我们自己，也包括所谓出身好一些的工农子弟和干部子弟都没有资格举菜刀。有那么几个小青年拉帮结伙，悄悄地成立了自己组织的菜刀队，夜袭队，游击队等，我们那拨儿孩子，有成立美洲虎队的。一经发现或被举报，立即被那些有权举菜刀，而且举过菜刀的人抓去，轻者解散，重者判刑。我所敬仰的一位年轻教师叫刘会国。有一天他来到我家，眼睛放着光，怀里揣着一把无比精致，无比锋利的短剑。跟出土文物有所不同的是，这把短剑的手柄是铜丝或漆包线缠出来的，金光闪闪。加上刀刃的银光闪闪，这是我迄今见过的最漂亮的一件冷兵器。我还拿过来掂了掂。嗯，儿童使用起来有些太重了。血气方刚，二三十岁的男子，如文质彬彬的青年教师刘会国，佩剑出行，应当是风光无限。刘先生拿刀刃部分自己比了比胸膛，胸膛厚度刚好从剑锋到剑柄的手环部分。也就是说，他这把短剑可以一剑刺穿胸膛，致人于死地。过了些天，传来凶信，刘会国老师以自杀结束了他年轻的生命。死因成谜。一个爱刀剑的好青年会自杀吗？他是我记忆当中在文革期间自杀的那一群人里面最年轻的。他辞世后去给他送葬火化的同事，同学们或称菜刀们对其尸体严重不恭，一头着地，不知道是头还是脚，另一头拖拉着他，丢进了焚尸炉。此举严重影响了后续自杀的人们。他们为了自己的尸首不遭此辱，有人就偷偷爬冶铁高炉的进料车，随它升到高炉的入料口，一千多度，烫死了事。这样做连一缕青烟都不会留下来。

　　什么样的羞辱？会让人产生自杀的念头，文革要销毁的人的尊严，不仅在他/她生前，还要在他/她死后。群众自杀了，叫自绝于人民，党员干部自杀了，叫自绝于党。这也包括被自杀的人们。我们还是回来说陈放先生的故事。陈放先生在他的批斗会上，衣衫不整，脖子上挂了一块硬纸壳做的牌子，用细棉绳或者细铁丝，编的是两个上角，挂在他的脖子上，牌子上写的是他的名字，用黑墨水，名字上面再用红墨水打一个大叉子。他的身体被两个家伙从后面一人一条胳膊的向后搋起，双臂在最高点，头和上身低着向前倾，双腿站在一把椅子上，保持这一姿势长达两小时之久，期间搋他的两个人被其他两人轮换上下场休息，而他老人家由于身体痛苦，又不能动，出大汗，流泪流鼻涕，弄了一脸，实在是惨不忍睹，这就是叫做坐土飞机。还有一个家伙，大概是发现他的知识量没有陈放先生那么多，当时谁的知识量大，读书多就叫喝多了墨水，少喝了几年墨水的人，在全校大会上，在2000多人面前，端起一盆墨水，迎头

泼向了手脚均被制伏不能动弹的陈放先生脸上。这种
羞辱，这种光天化日之下非人的折磨，这种反人类的罪
行，使陈放先生很快就承受不起，他用自杀的方式结束
自己的生命。但是他一介书生，手无缚鸡之力，想死都
死不掉。我从六岁起就把这段不公平藏在了心底，到我
成人的时候还是不能释怀，到了现在，在我父母已经双
亡，我自己已经人在海外，威胁我的这些菜刀们，老的
老了，死的死了，我的这种不安全感还是存在。我想该
轮到我出来说这件事儿了。要是不能拥有一点安全感，
那么大家一起不配拥有这个安全感，包括菜刀们。读
者自清，我说的潜在的威胁，以及再次爆发的文革，会
再现上述的情景，你怎么能够说服我？说服所有人，这
一切不会再有了，你上回是菜刀，回回是菜刀，难道下
一回还是菜刀吗？你上回是挨刀，回回都挨刀，难道不
会举一回菜刀吗？你麻木了吗？人类进化了吗？人类当
中的菜刀们进化了吗？人类这一部分菜刀最先进入农
耕，是不是还在那里择机而动？寻找一切倒退的可能，
一切退化的可能，而使自己变成一把菜刀，而进一步
掌握打人杀人的权力并且逍遥法外呢？这在没有法制
的地方是完全可能的，在原来有法制的地方，后来法
制被破坏的地方也是完全可能的。

　　1975年，我父亲从流放地回到钢院。所谓流放地，
就是钢院在河北省安平县办了一个"五七干校"。各个

单位都在外地办这个"五七干校"。因为毛在某年的5月7号作了指示啦,干部,教师分期分批下农村去接受劳动改造。这是俄国到苏联一贯实行的流放政治犯的中国翻版。比苏俄稍微好些的,有点改动的地方是,流放有期限,到期者回原单位。改造好了没有,不管。

我父亲就是一个没有改造好的典型。他回校一看,菜刀们上大学啦。这些上大学的菜刀们叫工农兵学员。他们没有什么学习能力,水平低下。我父亲就编排他们,调侃其大学的教学是"大学的招牌,中学的教材,小学的教法,幼儿园的脾气"。当天白天,学校的有线广播就开展了针对我父亲的新一轮大批判。当天夜里,我家的门再一次被菜刀敲开。我父亲刚开门,顺门缝就进来了一把如假包换的钢制菜刀。"程老师,我是来给你送菜刀的!"这就是工农兵学员在大学做过的菜刀级坏事之一。他们还逼迫大学教授们考试,考题由菜刀们命题。此当后话。后来,有些上过大学的菜刀们还做了官,当主席,当书记的,可高可大的官呢。

佛教相信轮回。

此生为人做事以善为先,死后立刻轮到来生,还是人。

此生为人,做了一些坏事,死后在地狱受些煎熬,之后才轮到来生,可能就不是人,轮回几次,屈指可数,还有机会再为人。

　　此生为人，做尽坏事，死后下到地狱，轮不到来生，轮回多少次都出不了地狱，受劫不可计数，没有机会再做人。叫做永世不得翻生。菜刀们的来生，就都是这样了。他们不会说话，无法沟通，不能把他们在另一个世界里所受的苦难和惩罚告诉后来的菜刀们，所以后生菜刀们不知道是什么样的惩罚与来生是个什么东西在另一个世界里等他们，他们不信教，不受戒，就继续作恶人，做坏事。无知者无畏。呵呵。你们等着吧！

　　基督教也劝善。好人上天堂，坏人下地狱。

　　有意思吧？

　　行善为本。

6
武斗

　　菜刀这个不上架的冷兵器，赶紧退场，下面来一段真的冷兵器。北京钢院是苏联莫斯科钢铁学院的翻版，上世纪50年代初建设，其功能不但教人用现代工业技术，冶铁炼钢，还叫人如何使用钢铁？铸造锻造粉末轧制等各种成型工艺，加上一点车钳焊铆切锯铣钻镗等机加工热处理，其校办工厂就可以生产刀具，到了文革武斗开始，就转产兵器，两派各自造兵器，有哪两派呢，文革一开始就开始分派，造反派和保皇派，而保皇派又是造反派对他们的对手的戏称，他们根本不保皇。各单位分派以后，又进行了一轮大联合，各单位的造反派联合到了一起叫天派，另一边也自动结合到了一起叫地派。地派在文革结束后，以亲近邓小平自居，马上夺取了各大专院校的领导权，那是后话，英语版本在这里加了巧克力说。现在接着说武斗，在大规模武斗爆发前夜，保皇派的一位学生，不明不白的死掉了，就在现在任何一种所大专院校当中，都应该是由校长亲自化解的重大事件。可是当时，连我们自己的校长高芸生，也已经自杀好久。他是用上级发给他的手枪，在自己的校长办公室里给了自己一枪，当场毙命，枪法时机等一切都无可挑剔的完美，但是自杀事件完美吗？可以用完美这个词吗？完结好吧。我现在是加拿大人，爱道歉。我要对"完美"这个词说抱歉。对于死掉的学生，在一所苏联专家援建的工业学院里，应该有一个比较科学的，令人信服的死因的说法，可是没有。两派双方各执一词，都指责对方打死人，嫁祸于对方，又都拿不出证据来，于是那两天的高音喇叭，广播车，在播音当中添上了新的可笑桥段，说死者是踩到面条上，滑倒而摔死，要打倒面条。又说他是踩到白菜帮子上滑倒摔死的，要打倒白菜。呜呼，人命关天，他们是以这种毫无严肃可言的小丑戏言，对人命关天事件，添加上去屈辱性的词，大肆广播宣传，此案今天有人翻吗？参与者，甚至可能是杀手，还活着吗？收尸，或者把这个悼词写成了打倒白菜，打倒面条的人，还在讲台上教书育人吗？我当时是六岁，最多七岁，七岁的我，在几乎百年无战事的北京城，（1860英法联军攻入北京，烧了皇家别墅群圆明园，算是有记载的最后一次战事，）却经历了一场又一场冷兵器和热兵器的交替战争，这是1967年的北京。钢铁学院的全部围栏，一种上面有铁矛尖, 两侧有下弯形的铁钩子, 后面一只长长的钢棍的钢铁制品, 被拿来做了长矛, 扎枪等兵器, 看看它的样子, 一枪扎进肚子, 在拔出来的时候, 后面可能两个钩子可以把肠子拉出来吧? 真够恐怖的, 很吓人, 再看看武装起来的学生, 青年教工们, 他们身穿护体的甲胄, 牛皮的帆布的, 头戴柳条帽, 那个时候没有钢盔, 用柳条编织而成的护头盔, 工作场所的劳动保护器具, 武斗的时候拿来做了头部护具, 当然, 脸部也有用击剑面罩类似的东西保护了起来, 浑身甲胄, 肩扛长矛。一个人照相的时候摆个古代武士普斯, 还可以, 算玩玩嘛。但是当一大帮子的人个个如此, 并且排着队, 喊着口号, "文攻武卫! 保卫延安! "延安公社, 就是钢院地派给自己起的名字。地院的同样派别称为东方红或者919, 温家宝在他的大学生时期, 就在这一派里, 该组织的头子王大宾被抓被判刑, 他倒没事, 后来还做了十年总理。他们以上战场的气势列队行进, 就算军队。这样通过我们的家属院落时, 就是恐怖了, 震撼了, 再淘气的孩子们也都灰溜溜的跑回家, 闭门关窗, 大气不喘的, 等待自己的末日到来。在那个年代, 菜刀破门抓人, 当着妻小的面殴打训斥大人, 把男的剃成光头, 让他成为外形上的罪犯, (我的汉字学恩师白迺桢, 笔名白化文先生受过此辱); 把女的剃成阴阳头, 就是一半头发去掉了, 留下另一半, 让她成为外形上的牛鬼蛇神, (我的高分子化学恩师单忠健女士受过此辱），门口走廊贴大字报，拉出去游街等等，一切行动都是那么可怕，再加上这个武装巡逻，我们是不是真的要完蛋了？反正我当时就是这么想，完了，活不过今天了。后来看电影，辛德勒的名单，当中有一幕重现1930-40年代纳粹德国镇压，驱赶犹太人的腾空犹太区之夜 （Aufreumung）。那是发生在1966-76中国文革之前30年，发生在外国的事情。再后来，发生在1966-1967中国文革50年后的2016-17年，北京市长蔡奇用刺刀见红为口号，在寒冷的冬天夜间，用冷兵器武装驱赶外地驻京经商人员，破坏他们的住所及店铺。人类文明一次又一次的被践踏，看看我们的邻居大院，那里更糟糕，清华大学东门内，有一处化学馆，它被火攻焚烧成一个骷髅，那里当时爆发了热兵器战事，推土机改造的土坦克上焊了钢板，谓之装甲，上面架起了机枪等火器，一种叫做燃烧瓶的热兵器大行其道，电石或者碳化钙成为抢手的军工器材原料。这里不便说，燃烧瓶的制作工艺，恐怖嫌疑嘛？实际上，当时七岁以上的孩子们都会做，所以我们小孩子们当时连空玻璃瓶子都弄不到手，因而无法制作，那才叫穷呢。清华大学爆发了互掷燃烧瓶和互相射击的热兵器武斗事件，被首钢的工人毛泽东思想宣传队，举着毛主席语录，喊破各方的防线，占领了清华大学，并由此开始了一次长达几年的，野蛮战胜文明的灾害，工宣队,军宣队占领校园,以及各大国营工厂,大专院校等,占领权力机构,凌驾于校长,书记以及一切职能管理部门之上,钢院,也被这样攻破了。各派熄火,向工宣队长宋永泉,及军代表金昭典投降。革造延安两派头头,都被结合进所谓的革命委员会,实行统治,这次行动叫做支左,支工,支农。从此,学校再也没有回到教职员工们的手里。直到今天,权力,仍然如此被野蛮化,即上级派谁来,谁就是这里的新主人,革命委员会拥有一切权力,而教职工代表大会,工会,学员,学者们毫无权力,只有一点点待遇,苟且偷安,何况在那个时候,哪里有安可偷? 处处危机,事情只以革命不革命区分,人只以敌我区分,钢院的权力中心移到了二斋,原来的大学生宿舍,后来的青年教工宿舍,现在是工宣队,军宣队驻扎的营地。这也揭开了钢院子弟势力范围的重新划分。

后来,到了1980年,1896年和1989年,直到1995年,我父亲三次合计5年,我母亲两次合计2年,我和我妻子骆辑各一次,合计12年到西德亚琛工业大学考察,进修,签约校际合作协议,客座工程师,联合培养,读研,看孙子,送孩子上大学附属幼儿园等项活动进行到细致入微,才了解到这所西方工业技术大学的运作及管理方式和财源,生源,毕业去向等问题是怎么做的。在这里仅将其管理阶层说明一下,给我的在中国各校当头头的同学读者看。其他读者可以跳过这一段。

西德北莱茵河西坡亚琛技术高校有三百多个研究所，每个所只有一名所长，他也是这个所的唯一教授。他和所有教授所长们，一人一票共同组成该大学的教授议会。还有一票是数万学生，包括博士生共同拥有。其他教职员工没有票。这个议会对该大学实行统治。从教授拥有票数（300）和教授占票率（300/301=99.7%）来看，这是绝对的教授治校。校长是教授议会的议长，他也只有一票，没有两票。2003年，我陪同清华大学赴西德（两德已经统一多年，应该叫德国了）海德堡大学考察团，在该校的哲学家小道上散步的时候，把上述亚琛大学的管理之道告诉了他们的随行教授（你们看看吧，中国教授在出访时只配作随行）。该团出资人是团长，清华紫光公司的一位女士。教授听懂了，让我再复述一遍给团长听。团长没听进去。呵呵。没听进去也没什么。人微言轻嘛。于是过了十几年，清华还是那样，书记治校，中国第一，其变化倒是有一个，清华在世界大学的排名滑坡了。

7

搬迁

回来说钢院。钢院在菜刀们的统治下出现了一次重大历史级机遇。它把钢院提升到了北京当时近百所高校的第三的位置。北大，清华，钢老三。话说1969年，老毛把跟他造党的反的学生们骗到农村去插队都有2年多了。"广阔天地，大有作为"。"知识青年到农村去，接受贫下中农的再教育，很有必要"。1969年中，老毛又把在北京的高校迁址到农村，从北大清华搬家开始，他们都去江西。钢院也计划去江西，连我父亲都被派去当第一批先遣队，以往要彻夜排队才能买到的火车票现在是有人买好了送到家里。几块不刨不漆的薄木板钉成箱子，外面捆了稻草秆拧成的草绳，防震其次，防箱子破裂为主，根本不防潮，也不防水。第二天赶火车的父亲也不跟我们话别，因为是要去"戴罪立功"的前夕。那个时候，我弟弟刚出生，还不到半岁。半夜里，门被快速而不失悦耳地轻轻敲开了。来人报告了一个好消息，伟大领袖毛主席听从了他在北京市革命委员会（当时该委员会夺了市委市政府不听毛主席的话的彭真的权，成为北京市最高领导团伙）安插进去的主任谢富治的意见，华北还是需要一个钢铁学院的。于是指示钢院原地不动，取消搬迁计划。这个最新最高指示居然没有文字版记载，奇。其实在中国这个没有任何文字记载的事，物，比比皆是。中国共产党在哪里注过册？它的各个机构又在哪里注过册？它的花费，占用，从来都是非法违规的签字报销的，叫做白条。此话另有专门的章节。同是钢院子弟的穆军有个周恩来版本如下：1969年3月2号，中苏边境乌苏里江的珍宝岛上两国军队打起来了。第一，坐实了苏修社会帝国主义亡我之心不死；第二，缴获了一辆苏制坦克。把它从冰冻的江水里打捞上来，其装甲部分拆解下来，就到了钢院金属材料研究室。人家老修的钢是怎么炼的？不光是硬，它还韧。火箭弹，反坦克炮弹打上去，就如同老师的粉笔在黑板上点了一个点，被炮炸过的整体装甲钢板不破不裂。穆军之父穆成璋教授主持这项准军工研究，半夜不回家，被周恩来总理来探班时叫去汇报了。穆老先生请总理放心，这种复合金属装甲材料一定能够研发出来，但是要假以时日。政务院周恩来总理听完穆教授的汇报后，再去向军委毛泽东主席汇报时，他们商定留下钢院在北京，不随其他院校搬迁。于是钢院就幸运地留在了首都，成为全国冶金类大专院校之首。其实，北京钢院的业务水平北不如在沈阳的东北工学院，南不如在长沙的中南矿冶学院。只是因为这个和平时期没有搬迁，准备打仗需要钢铁而没有完全中断技术研发（学术？从来就没有学术。呵呵），　使得校址和水准都原地不动的钢院在其他院校折腾搬迁引发教学研究中断而倒退时凸显了出来。

8
家庭经济

文革前后的家庭经济生活是怎样的呢？没有银行。工资以单位为发放源头。每个月一次。通过现金的形式。父母上班工作的地方一般都叫单位。中国是中央集权制，分个上层建筑和经济基础，这个地方高级到上层建筑的院，区，市，省局，部，委，等就改名叫做机关了，或者叫院里，区里，市里，省里，局里，部里。这个地方低级到经济基础的县，农场，工厂，公社，生产队，等就又改名叫做地方了，或者叫县里，场里，厂里，社里，队里了。1994年中国商业部长吴仪女士带数百人大团到德国访问，有一位德方首席翻译小伙子，金发碧眼的德国人就精彩地口译出这个那个"里"，让我这个同样同场作翻译的中国人都自叹不如。单位里发工资这一天，财务科就准备了一抽屉的钱，每人每份都是预算好了，分放现金好了，扎结在一个多孔纸带上，细细的属于你的那条纸带上，蘸水钢笔字体手写写着房租多少，水

254

电多少, 统筹医疗多少, 连租用的家具租金多少都在上面。真是给自己看的, 实发工资多少, 都包装在这个纸带里了, 分毫不差。各个领工资的人拿到18元到240元。文革时期十年没浮动过。挨整的人倒是有被扣全部工资, 每个月发放18元生活费的, 后来死了的, 活着的都有一些, 不是全体, 又补发工资的所谓"落实政策"一说。我的大姨父张善先先生就经历了这一次, 他从文革伊始被整成汉奸叛徒资本家, 到调查结论出来, 他是新四军地下医药用品供应线在上海的线民及自制药品, 自费供应新四军的爱国的民族资本家, 他是被日本宪兵队抓去酷刑折磨到永远失去生育能力也没有背叛中国军民的抗日地下活动的抗日真好汉, 他在文革中期就马上被"落实了政策", 并且补发了每月几百元的工资, 恢复原职, 仍然任北京化工总厂的总工。这个北京化工总厂, 就是张善先先生在1950年代公私合营时全部献给国家的上海一心化学厂迁京才有的北京化工。而此前北京就没有化工。大姨父用补发的工资数千元在北京东四北大街南吉祥胡同15号里买了一排带家具的北房。原屋主是印尼华侨, 在1949回国后至文革中受尽了苦难, 文革还没结束, 就设法到海外, 全家搬出了北京, 远离了中国。现在用这几千元, 在同样地段买同样的房子是不可能的。恐怕连半个平米都买不到。有人有读者可能质疑, 文革期间买卖房子? 怎么可能? 我告诉你和所有的读者，这是真的。卖方是著名归国华侨，后又逃离中国，现在叫先海归，又归海，政策网开一面，可以卖房。买方是纯粹的爱国民族资本家，中国化工在那时候上海第一，上海他第一，技术第一，外国人连一点股份，技术，设备，市场都没有，而且他建的化工厂全部献给了新中国。这是硬核。政策又网开一面，可以买房。这是一个特殊的例子。更加普遍的是拿十几块几十块工资的人怎么养家？下面介绍一下家庭经济紧巴巴的，过不了日子的时候，第二经济来源就成了重头。这叫做工会补贴。每一个领工资的人都是工会会员。会员的家里是他一个人领工资挣钱，七八个人吃饭的，就绝对属于工会发放补贴的对象。因为一个人的工资全部用来买米买面买白薯白菜的话，都确实不够。我给大家演算一下就清楚了。一斤（500克或者半公斤）面粉0.185元，全家定量的20%可以买这种白面粉。所谓定量是配给制。粮食定量从初生婴儿的每个月20斤到成年人每个月30斤（15公斤或者33磅）。配给制当中各种票证有面票，米票，粮票，油票，还有一个购货本，每个月一页纸，凭本可以购买限量的副食，如鸡蛋每户每月2斤，猪肉每人每月1.5斤，牛羊肉？根本不卖给汉人，只供应回民。鸡鸭鱼虾是过年排大队才能买到的东西。1980年春节前，我的媳妇就是露天排队数小时买冻鸡冻鸭冻鱼的时候，给去晚了的我妈妈，她的大学老师，认识不到半年，一

个空位，让她少挨三小时的冻，从而结了善缘，变成我
媳妇的。糖每人每月0.5斤，粉丝三两，芝麻酱每户每月
2两（100克），花生油每人每月0.5斤，豆腐每户每月2斤
或者十块等，还有每人每年布不到14尺（不到3米），棉
花不到3斤。这些东西能买到并且买足份量就不错了。
经常是一个月一年都过去了，卖副食的小店，叫合作社
的地方供货不足，这些定量就过期作废了。我家厨房
的窗户对着钢院里面的合作社，只要那边有动静，来货
了，我是从厨房窗户跳出去，飞一般跑到合作社去排队
的前十名，后面跟着一路小跑的我姐姐，走正道，拿着
购货本和钱。我从9岁到15岁就干这个"家务"，所以身
手不凡，跳高，短跑，障碍赛什么的都有两下子。回来
说粮店，南方叫米店。有户口的人都有定量，从出生到
死亡都有，每个月十几斤到最高35斤。一个6口之家，每
个月买面要40元；买米每斤0.152元，好大米每斤0.213
元，这家买米也要花30元；买棒子面，每斤0.112元，15
元得花吧？这粮食一项开支就85元。没有肉吃的年代
人人饭量大，家里男孩多的粮票都用掉了还是不够吃
的，就设法弄粮票。我从7岁小学一年级到15岁初中二
年级，每年都去当童工时，学校逼迫我们全体同学去
做一天，一周甚至一个月的轻重体力劳动，却从不给
我们发工资，而是事后每人每天发给0.5斤粮票补助一
下。要说明一下的是，这还不是自己设法多弄粮票，多

吃多占, 而是形势所迫, 大家一起, 必须去学工, 学农, 学军, 学商。家里女孩多, 并不缺粮食吃的女生也都得停课去劳动。14, 15岁的女孩子们经期腰腹痛, 校方, 就是带队下乡去劳动的头头谢国栋, 而不是老师们不管不顾, 照样要求她们跟男生们一样, 赤足下水田去插秧, 拔草, 时间长了站不住哇, 于是我的可怜的女同学们高高地挽起裤腿, 跪在泥巴浑水里劳作, 牛虻, 蚂蝗, 水蛭什么的, 攀附在我们的没多少肉也没有多少血的瘦腿上。这里原谅我吧! 我实在写不下去了。我们疼不堪, 苦不堪, 居然没有人代言反抗说, 这样不可以。

前面说到, 一个6口之家每个月要花85元买粮食, 还不一定够吃。85元是什么工资级别哪? 我爸爸那时候当大学讲师, 中级职称里面的最高等待遇, 每个月才89.50元。他要养6口人的我们家是不可能的。幸亏有我妈妈, 她那个时候在大学也当讲师, 每个月能拿78元呢。总之, 其他人养不了家的就去工会申请补贴。每人每个月的补贴高限是30元, 底线是零, 工会的会员费大概是每个月0.13元吧。你敢不听话? 你敢不说社会主义好? 不说共产党好? 你敢不说毛主席是人民的大救星? 说了就拿不到补贴, 取消补贴, 就是让这家别活了。所以忠于不忠于党的政治倾向说到底是经济问题在那里, 是家庭经济问题在那里。你有半点意见, 对党国不忠不爱, 等着吧! 饿死你!! 还没说冻死你呢!!! 因为配给制连棉花和布都要票,有定量的。每人每年3斤棉花票,14尺布票。这点东西够做棉袄的就不够做棉被的,做了冬衣就别惦记夏天的短袖衫了。皮袄?在顺口溜里,而不在现实的生活里。

哥俩好,哥俩好

哥俩上街买皮袄

你冬天穿,我夏天穿

○○○○○○

羽绒服?那时候还没发明哪。所以棉花是唯一可以御寒的服装材料。背心?没听说过。穿背心露肩了就不许上学了,所以干脆不穿背心,光肚皮外面穿一件体面一点的中山装。我的个子较大,从小就被人戏称为费布票,浪费粮食。家里给一般人做的棉被不够我从头盖到脚的。冬夜里卷缩成一团在6-7摄氏度的朝北的房间里睡一夜,家里其他4口人都挤着睡到南屋去了,第二天早上醒来醒不来,全靠我的姐姐进北屋探视一下。出被窝可是一种挑战。我的上身穿了一件出口援非物资,就是一件质地非常好的海军蓝圆领长袖绒衣。绒衣给非洲人穿未免太捂得慌,人家不要,就转内销了,6元一件啊。我穿了一年又一年,个子长大了,胳膊长长了,绒衣好像缩水了一般,不能再外穿了,就当内衣穿,最后长袖变成了短袖,它还象新的一样,连开线,褪色都没有。为什么要支援世界革命啊？先让我出被窝别马上冻得抽筋就行。鸡皮疙瘩天天起，这不是病，是穷的。在这种饥寒交迫的生活支配下，还搞什么阶级斗争，路线斗争，还提什么社会主义实践，共产主义理想？全是骗人的。实质上是在搞补贴奴隶制。你不听主人的，就吃饭穿衣什么也没有，你自己还没地方弄食儿去。你听从主人的话了，也没有比别人多半点物资。你的衣食所得仅仅够你维持半温不饱的，你得不停地要要要，就必须一直听话听话听话，向党表忠心。

我有个邻居，是钢院印刷厂的排字工人李友仁，钢院几千号人，姓李的多了，他却独占江湖，外号小李子。他是钢院职工足球队的守门员，平时穿一条料子裤，蹬一辆锰钢涨闸全链套转铃儿的新自行车。现在叫做帅呆了，以往叫做酷毙了，当时就叫做顽主。顽主在钢院公开的一次是1970年的联合国由中国替代中华民国，各单位庆祝会上，钢院印刷厂全体职工上台表演一个集体诗朗诵之类的节目。小李子当大反派，就是美国驻联合国代表。你看他指着中华民国代表的鼻子骂出诗意来：

讨厌讨厌真讨厌
你的脸色不好看
人家上厕所
你也跟着转

。。。。。。

可笑的是，为了丑化美国人，李叔叔给他自己的脸上涂了一层兰不兰绿不绿的颜色，上台却说别人脸色不好看。到了1985年我在矿院北京研究生部第一次见到一个标致的美国人，美国能源署署长，犹他大学教授John A. Herbst的时候，我把他和我亲爱的李叔叔扮演的美国佬在内心作了对比，嗯，哪儿都像，就是脸色不像。

回来说李叔叔。他和他超指标生儿子的故事好像是我记忆当中唯一的例外，家庭经济学在文革中的例外。我们家和李叔叔他们家住在一个单元门里，5栋110，我家6口占两间小屋，每一间14平方米，他家5口，占一个大屋，18平方米，两家共用一个厨房，一个蹲坑式有抽水冲便水箱无洗手池的厕所，苏联标准哈。这么挤着住在一起，亲密如一家人。李叔叔带我去石油学院游泳池游泳，在那里教会了我换气憋气。从此回到钢院的游泳池去打水仗，就是在水中双方互相往对方脸上泼水，不许身体有接触的游戏，我还真的没输过。这样几个冬夏过去，李叔叔的爱妻李阿姨生啊生，先生了俩女儿，又怀上了第三胎。这回是男的。但是这就破坏了全钢院的计划生育。李叔叔因此被停发了工资，工会的补贴也被停了。全家没有了生计，家里还供养着李叔叔的丈母娘的妈妈呢，叫丈母姥姥呗，她老人家从山西来，足不出户，帮衬着做点家务，照看重孙女，顺便还教会了我这个重孙子辈儿的邻居做葱油饼，我烙的饼是老山西正传，讲究外焦里嫩，葱不糊，面不淡，细数那个层，多达到9，是极数。别吹了。李叔叔家要断顿儿了，就是没饭吃了。单位不给工资，工会不给补贴，工会的会员们可不干了。他们用外快来赞助工友加哥们小李子。什么外快呢？收电影票。大一点的单位自己放电影，在露天平坦广阔的地方支两根电线杆，挑一块白布，电影片从电影发行公司借，不要钱。钢院的放映场最早设在丁家大院外，大操场的西北角，这个丁家大院以后有详细介绍。后来电影放映室因为是个独立的小房子，离住宅远，就改做液化石油气供应站。而电影放映场则搬到大饭厅外，大操场的正南了，这里可以容纳更多的观众，白布屏幕的两面都有观众，这收门票的事就落到工会会员们的手里了，是一件除了每天8小时正式工作以外的捞外快的工作，还不是天天都有，最多每周一次吧。观众每人交5分钱，彩色电影，宽银幕电影，外国电影可能要1毛钱。小李子是工会活动积极分子，放电影时去维持秩序，拉起绳子圈地，隔几十米一个入口，收收门票，李叔叔每场都去。放电影是工会发放的福利。一帮他的哥们，都是工会活动的积极分子收了门票以后，自己一分不留，全掏出来聚在一堆里，钢蹦儿多，毛票儿少，哗啦啦倒给了小李子。2千观众每人5分钱，也是100

块呀! 那段时间, 全钢院的人以此声援小李子, 救援小李子。我们放最新潮的电影, 重放最受欢迎的老电影, 几乎达到每周一次的电影夜场, 使钢院喜获" 体育电影学院" 的雅号。被计划生育这个国策击中的李叔叔, 意外地收获了工友情, 而我们大家观赏了当时可以发行的全部电影, 无一漏看, 无一个孩子缺席。苦难的童年, 加上了李叔叔们, 让我们因祸得福不浅。大家知道什么叫跑片子吗? 就是几个场同时上映同一本电影拷贝。当然, 这个同时是有一到两卷拷贝的时间差的。在这个时间差里, 一位摩托车手, 在两个场子之间来回运拷贝, 就叫做跑片子。物质贫乏的年代, 一部电影拷贝在同一个夜晚跑片子两个或更多场, 能娱乐多少在日间受苦受难的普罗大众啊。每一句经典台词, 每一个人物, 都在我们幼小的心里占据着不可替代的位置, 也是永远不会忘记的欢乐颂。直到今天, 我们聚会时, 还在不停地演绎这些东西。

一个李向阳, 把你吓成这个样子?

托马大叔是军官, 他还让我当军官

张军长, 请你看在党国的份上, 伸出手来, 拉兄弟一把

你的真正的军人的不是, 战术的不懂

随手拈来, 脍炙人口。最得意的是革命歌曲改版唱, " 打靶歌" 变成了如下曲艺, 翻版的是文革电影"

青松岭",正面人物一个也记不住,反面人物总共有仨,一个也没落下:

钱广赶大车孙富捎点儿货,

榛子,辣椒还有蘑菇。

钱广的老婆心眼多,

"你为什么多给他两块多?"

钱广说:"这就是,羊毛出在羊身上。"

钱广的老婆一撇嘴,

一下泼了钱广一脸水,

嘿!泼他一脸水!

秋冬交季,第一场薄雪来之匆匆。地里的作物大规模地进入钢院这样的大单位。都有些什么呢?白薯,白菜,大葱。还有就是煤。其规模之大,不是一般马车驴车三轮车能拉进来的,而是用带拖斗的十轮大卡拉来的。十轮大卡车,是我们的孩提时代,1960-1970能见到的最大卡车了。国产的8吨的黄河,4吨的解放都不行,要捷克的泰特拉才行。马达一响,动力澎湃,进入钢院不太宽的北门,经过家属区,钢院为之沸腾。1,2,3,4栋那个院子的东侧,到合作社院子的西侧的空场地上,排满了排队的孩子们。有时需要彻夜排队。家里的几个孩子轮流排,不可以加三儿的。白菜由人工摆成传送链,一棵一棵地传递下车,白薯用几股钢叉或者一麻袋一麻袋地搬运下车,堆放到地上,然后才开始卖。一斤粗粮票可以买5斤白薯。粮食总是不够吃的饥荒问题每年有一次缓解，就发生在白薯进入每个家庭的时刻。穷家要进500斤以上，富家也要进100斤，当时的贫富差别也就是5倍吧。今天何止千倍万倍？！白薯这个东西即怕冻又怕捂还怕潮，所以还要窖藏，不能简单地放在屋里的地板上，床铺下面。于是钢院的小块空地上纷纷支起了一个一个菜窖白薯窖的出入口，各家一个，绝不兼容。我们班最能干的同学黄陆军一天能挖5个菜窖。他50岁不到，却已经早早离开了人世，估计是他从小体力透支，劳累过度而疫而终的吧？他不仅给自己家挖菜窖，还给老师，同学，邻居家挖，上冻之前连续挖个不止。家属院子里，两棵树之间在这时候往往拉上一条又一条的绳子，上面串了一串串的白薯干，讲究一点的还是先蒸后凉的白薯干呢！此时绝无偷盗行为，私有制还是受到一些尊重的，仅仅在共度饥荒的最低档食物这个层面上。此情此景一直延续到1980年代的中期，钢院食堂也在公共浴室附近大肆建筑地面菜窖，里面储藏了大量白菜，以十轮大卡整车整车地计算。我们中学英语课本里，就有对此景象的英语短语，叫做"bumper harvest"，大丰收。欢乐的景象以不太体面的狂欢收场：1981年吧？中国女排在此季节夺取世界冠军。那时候各个学生宿舍都已经配备了黑白电视机，叫匈牙利19吋。同学们把系学生会掌管的电视机架在一层楼窗前，屏幕朝窗外，这样全系数百名同学都可以观看实况转播。观众人群的旁边，就是这些白菜，刚刚卸载到地面，还没有来得及入窖，或者是倒白菜，就是把白菜从菜窖里搬出来晒太阳，减低其外在水分。这边电视机里的女排胜利的画面刚刚出现，钢院食堂冬储大白菜就全部飞上了天。当然，这是激动万分的大学生们狂欢所致。这年冬季白菜短缺，食堂的熬白菜这种1毛一份的最便宜的大锅菜也趁机涨价，到了1毛5一份，并且再也没有落回去。更加欢乐的是，女排听说此事后，居然派北京女排，当时也是全国冠军，专程来钢院秀了一秀。钢院大学生男排迎战，只打十分，变换了十种战术的北京女排胜出，强攻，背溜，短平快，加三儿，前飞，背飞，后排，封网，二次，探头什么都会。钢小伙们实际上只会高举高打一种战法，还因为吃不饱，吃不好，尽管他们每天比普通学生多吃一份0.40元的营养餐，还是柔而不刚则败。而北京队的姑娘们，她们每人的伙食标准在当时是上百元/月。穷文富武啊。女篮宋小波，女排郎平都跟我同一届。她们多高？184公分以上，我还是男的大个子呢，身高才180公分。

食物是不够的，百姓是挨饿的，冬季挨饿是感觉到寒冷的。每年11月15日，到次年3月15日，要由钢院锅炉房向所有楼房供暖，叫做集中供暖，供的是水暖。为此，钢院每年进大约数千吨的无烟煤。煤也是由大型卡车泰特拉运来的,连续几天运煤才能堆起一座煤山。然后由外面招募来的锅炉工昼夜24小时不停地烧煤换热水。有那么两年,我父亲挨整,堂堂的大学讲师不能去讲台授课。当然,即没有招生,也就没有学生听课。那么我父亲挨整的具体内容,就是去锅炉房烧锅炉。烧的那个锅炉落后至极,要人工运煤,投料,出渣,添冷水,抽热水。算一算他的体力劳动的运动量吧:成百上千吨煤要从煤堆旁铲到手推车里,推到锅炉边,一铲一铲地扬进去,再把燃料煤10-20%的灰渣扒出锅炉,装上手推车,运到渣堆去倒掉。每天各位锅炉工的手工装卸量在十吨,一点都不夸张。班次是12小时/班,休息24小时,也就是说他每天都要倒时差,外加强体力劳动,环境脏乱差,高危险,几乎每年都会发生锅炉爆炸,民工死伤的钢院锅炉房,院内没有比这份"工作"再低贱的了。我都怀疑菜刀们要借锅炉爆炸弄死我爸爸了,可是他人致贱则无敌,不但挺了过来,还练就了他能不论何时何地,倒头便可以入睡,而且从来不睡过头的奇门"本领",彻底告别困扰知识分子的抑郁症,神经衰弱,睡不着觉的亚健康,他变成了身心两健的"劳动人民"。至于他以及其他在钢院锅炉房从事劳动改造的大小知识分子们为什么一个都没有被炸死炸伤? 这可以感谢他们所拥有的由科学技术知识武装起来的大脑吧。以我父亲为例,他是物理化学专家,专业在于通过热力学三定律跟热量，温度，压力打交道，从数字到实践，伺候个把炉子，包括烧开水的锅炉还真是他的强项呢。这部分知识民工就不具备，往往是误操作锅炉还不知不觉，才导致事故的发生的。回来说我们的冬季取暖。距离锅炉房近的住所的暖气比较热，散热片上基本上不能用手摸，太烫；而距离锅炉房远的住所暖气比较凉，散热片达不到室温，当然也不到人体的体温，还要采人体之暖。那里的居民如何过冬呢？太阳能。不要搞笑，真的是初级太阳能。那么太阳能是如何进入卧室的呢？是我们的棉袄棉被在出太阳的日子里，拿到室外去接受阳光的直接照射，下午趁着太阳最足，气温最高的时候把棉被捧回家，当晚这个棉被之宣和柔软，散发出一种人体汗，尿，和太阳紫外光合成的骚味。你体验一把，会爱上这种味道的。我还绝对不是个变态。

贫困和利用贫困的事情，笔者认为，利用贫困打压别人是魔鬼的行为，而在贫困中自求平和乃至快乐是人的社会性以及美好的一面。

文革当中搭窝热潮大约有三次。

第一次是建筑防空洞。核武器空袭的威胁近在咫尺，中苏边境离中国首都北京最近的地方仅有300公里。苏联在蒙古驻扎军队。这一点在我1989年6月1日乘火车路过蒙古国首都乌兰巴托时亲眼验证过。大批苏联士兵和军官有的徒手，有的手提一个密码公文箱，在火车站为他们专用的站台整建制地进进出出。60年代末70年代初以苏联红军携带核弹头打击中国战略目标之首,即被列出北京第一。坦克攻入中国到达北京也只是一天之内的事,所以要人人建防空洞,藏身洞,家家在玻璃窗上贴米字纸,据说是在空袭中震碎了的玻璃可以伤人,而贴了米字纸的玻璃在成为玻璃碴以后会耷拉在窗户框上,减少或者不会漫天飞了伤人。这一招大概从二战中学来的,日本轰炸中国,德国空袭伦敦,当地百姓都是这样御敌的。人在空袭中要躲起来,防空洞的建筑水平天差地远了去了。钢院在1, 2, 3, 4栋南边大操场的西北角上占了一块地,围上铁丝网,里面堆满了建筑材料。人员,施工等均由一个姓丁的老干部负责,因此该围栏内被钢院人戏称为丁家大院。钢院附小校长艾亚文先生在文革一开始就被"揪"了出来,批倒下台,当了丁老头或者老丁头的唯一伙计。苏修的威胁大了,全钢院的人都在挖防空洞,脱坯,制砖,烧窑,构筑钢筋混凝土的弓形预制块;而当苏修威胁小了的时候,全钢院仅一人继续施工防空洞,打夯,挖土,排水,筛砂等,这个人就是艾亚文校长,叫做戴着反革命的帽子接受人民群众的监督,劳动改造。任何人都可以一人,或者纠集几个人对艾校长在防空工事施工现场展开批斗,指着他的鼻子骂他。我一个7, 8岁的小屁孩去挖得很深的大沟里从上往下偷偷窥视他,或者叫探视他，反而被他认作是去监督他，向单位方面反映，报告他不老老实实接受劳改的小特务。这个是一个误解。他是无监督状态独自劳改的，而我父亲是有监督，与众多劳改人员一起，正从干热的砖窑里往外背砖呢。砖窑就在金物楼的西南角，现在是腐蚀楼或者金相楼所在地。钢院当时仅有的四位中科院院士魏寿昆，肖纪美，柯俊和一位住在院外的大学问家，他们在文革初期也被迫去劳改，而他们共同的劳改地点是金属物理楼4个楼层的厕所，劳改内容是保洁每层楼的男女厕所。这8个厕所马上成为全钢院的人都愿意去"朝拜"的地方，因为院士们扫厕所的态度是科研探索精神的延伸，他们通过实践和交流，把拖把洗过，但是当天不用，而是到了拖把快风干了的时候才用来擦地，结果是地面干干净净。你们看干净干净，这俩汉字让仓颉造的，让院士们理解的：干就是无水，净就是少一点水。对吧？院士们保洁的厕所都是最干净的，难怪人们都要去"朝圣"。

第二次稍微有规模的建筑搭窝小高潮真是小得不能再小了。就是建小厨房，小花园，小鸡窝等。人们越生孩子越多，可是钢院这样的单位已经有好几年不盖房子了，多出来的人住到哪里去，就有了上述的小厨房，小花园，小鸡窝的建筑小高潮，这多为住一楼的人们自动扩大居住面积所为。把家里的厨房拓成卧房，拆掉炉灶安放床给孩子们住。厨房就搬到了室外。窗前一小片地被围起来，里面什么都有，灶，花盆，小鸡笼，蛐蛐罐，拉几条凉衣服绳等等。室内也慢慢地被租住在这里的人家把租用的家具换成了自制的沙发，一对单人沙发，带上茶几。我的小表哥萨本仁还给他的妈妈，我的大姑程述舜，制作了一张席梦思床，带钢丝绷网，钢丝压簧的，正宗的席梦思单人床。这是我们家最高级的床了。我也因此学习了西方家具制作过程和制作标准。毕竟财力有限，这件家具的制作时间超长，我表哥是每个月18元的学徒工资，而一个压簧却要4-5元，一张单人床怎么也要40-50个压簧吧？木框，面料，工具等都不算，也得200多块呀。

第三次建筑热潮是1976年的唐山大地震后，钢院以及华北地区忽然冒出了一批抗震棚，没有一间是重样的，也没有一间是按图纸建筑的。全是民间高手，一拍脑袋想想就造了。居然没有一间倒塌，完全抗住了后来的余震。其中我家的抗震棚是我自己一个人亲手建筑的。一根梁，就是一条长长的厚木板，横陈竖起在两根水泥杆上，水泥杆就是拉铁丝网用过的网柱。柱子顶头上压横梁，在民间叫做"猴儿顶灯"。猴子嘛，灵活而不耐压，压力来了它会跑的。这种结构冠名"猴儿顶灯"就是说它不可靠，不结实的意思。抗震棚里的"床"正好在钢院地下走暖气管道的水泥方形管路，冬暖夏凉。地面是土，墙面不能只是土，要黄土和石灰混成夯实，其工艺叫做"干打垒"。为了这个看似普通而且价廉的，但是当时不但抢手，罕见，而且难得的建筑材料石灰，我去弄了一辆双轮手推车，半夜偷盗了我的母校，钢院附小的仅有的一吨存货，结果因为这辆破车是漏的，一路漏下来的石灰象田径运动场上的跑道线一样，从仓库直到我家的抗震棚以及另外两个同案犯家的抗震棚划出供完美破案的铁证。附小杂役班伯伯半夜惊醒，他家就住在附小楼里。他悄悄跟了我们一路好几趟，取证完整。于是案发，我们仨一起上了钢院十字路口的通报栏。钢院十字路口可是个大地方，文革以来数次大字报高潮都在那里首先糊上墙，那时候的所谓大字报墙也是临时建筑，高粱秆的皮之类的农作物编成席，钉在木桩木条凑合出来的框子上，顶部还搭了防雨檐来。这些虽然也是建筑材料，但是我们几个淘气过头的孩子们以及其他孩子们谁都不敢去弄那些东西。政治相关的东西，弄坏了就惹大祸了，叫做破坏文革，破坏伟大领袖毛主席的战略部署，现行反革命，这些罪名不但会毁掉你自己，还会诛连你全家。其实，钢院附小的仓库位于其操场的东北角上的一处积肥站内。严格来说，那里的石灰就是为了固化或者碱化积肥场的地面而准备的。在硬化的地面上泼上人粪便，那都是从各个单位，包括钢院粪井里淘出的稀汤臭水, 用马车拉到那里放出来的真正的有机肥料。这些臭东西用太阳能晒干, 成就一块一块龟裂的粪块。唉! 我们上的小学真是臭不可闻。这都是真的。那时候的蔬菜绝不可以生吃。原因就是它们都是经过这种人粪便肥料的催肥成长, 其表面有洗不掉的细菌, 大肠杆菌等, 生吃了它们形同痢疾病菌, 甲肝病毒直接入口, 还不如直接吃屎哪! 进入西方后, 我几乎天天在家做饭炒菜。我所使用的食材, 特别是蔬菜, 不论是地面生长的叶子还是地下结块的, 藤上挂的, 无水栽培的, 我是从来不洗, 凉拌热炒, 切了就烹, 却从来没有吃坏过肚子。这个巨大的差别, 你们看到了吗? 为什么中国人民一定要喝烧开过的水, 而西方这边的人, 不论是瓶装水还是自来水, 一律打开就喝, 都是出于这个因素, 源头就有问题是不行的, 说出来了甚至恶心人, 恶心到要死了的地步。

写点轻松的吧。

文革中我作为一个在都市的单位里生长的男孩, 要做的家务有: 搬煤, 挖菜窖, 倒白菜, 领牛奶, 买馒头窝头, 买米背面, 切菜砍瓜, 等等。先说搬煤。钢院的西北角上有个型煤厂, 生产煤粉加土加石灰加水等做出来的蜂窝煤和煤球。蜂窝煤由冲压机压制而成, 而煤球由双辊对转机械轧制而成。去煤厂看这两部机器的运转也是件好玩的事, 后来成为工科男的我, 受到这个煤加工机械的启发和影响有多少，不知道。反正就是对工业机电相关的东西感兴趣，包括汽车，与对我所学的化工相比，对机电更感兴趣。生产出来的煤球还好，由机械传送带运走堆放库房，全自动化哈。而生产出来的蜂窝煤就要煤厂的工人，男女各半吧，用手搬到手推车上，推到晾晒场的地陇旁，在用手码到陇上，间隔稍大，走风祛水，使蜂窝煤变干变硬，可以称做煤饼了，然后再用手搬到三轮平板车上，由女工拉着，她根本骑不动，蹬不动，每车几百块啊，大的小的，还有几块草的，就是煤粉中混入锯末草芥等易燃引火物，用于生火，把耐燃的煤饼点燃。几百块煤就这么由一个女工拉着一辆三轮平板车，来到家属住宅的楼下，再由她用手卸载，一家一堆的码好，一块不多，一块不少，外观可计数的，收了钱，蹬上三轮车，独自回厂去了，她得一天拉好几趟，命苦了去了。此后再从楼门口搬进自己家的堆煤地点，就是我的家务劳动了。看到一小堆蜂窝煤上有一块煤饼上面用白色粉笔写了我家的门牌号码，我的人生就有了如此具体的意义：从第一块到最后一块全是我一个人负责无破损地搬回家。诗和远方都不在，薄膜唱片的唱机也得停转，英语灵格风唱片收入纸袋中，我得搬煤砖去了。首先在平地上放两块煤饼，在它们的上面放置一个叫做搓板，洗衣板的木头板，再在板上码三到四块煤饼，然后象砌砖一样错开码放多层煤饼，搬起来走路，上楼梯都尽量不要碰到衣服，叫做悬腕托盘搬运，这个动作须用更大的臂力。煤是黑的，蹭到衣服上还得洗衣服，自己洗自己的衣服，鞋袜，又多了一份家务劳动。讲究干净的家务搬运工们，在煤饼上盖一个围裙，就可以用胸膛和肚子掂着煤饼。电梯，洗衣机？没有！我放四层煤饼已经是我的体能极限了，一趟16块呀！我是个孩子啊！有一次搓板歪了一下，煤饼摔碎了几块，从此就弃之不用，而是改用木制的凳子翻过来搬煤饼。凳子的撑子和凳子腿都形成了围栏作用，保护了煤饼，却累坏了我。因为凳子也是有自重的，它比搓板重多了，而可搬运煤饼的数字却没有上升。这么着每个月一次，每次150-200块煤饼。每天每个炉灶要加4-5块大煤饼。煤灰铲，铁簸箕，通条，大小一套几个铸铁炉圈和取放它们的铁钩子，你们都见过吗？见过的都50岁以上了。文革后期，1976年吧？液化石油气罐子和灶具进入钢院，每个月还是一次，去换那个几十公斤重的铁罐子。别人家都是全家出动，一人搭一把手，其中一人在前面推着自行车，后面跟俩扶着罐子，其实罐子已经捆绑在自行车的后货架上了，不扶也不会掉下车去，可是它重呀，重得可能把车弄翻了。我还是一个人干这件家务。把那个几十公斤重的铁罐子往自行车后货架的弹簧夹子上一夹，不用绳子捆，因为捆的功夫，自行车的重心就可能歪到一边去，而把整车带翻的。左脚认蹬，右脚点地加速，然后一骈腿上车，我骑着自行车去换煤气罐。有一次这个只夹着没捆着的煤气罐就从后货架上掉下去了，在钢院的柏油马路上骨碌骨碌地滚到了路边的排水沟里，那时候沟里是土，或者泥巴。没事。我笑嘻嘻地捡起罐子，夹到车上继续前进。可笑，可怜的是，几个路过的人，不分大人还是孩子，走避不及，有的卧倒，有的弯腰，估计他们的腿已经不听从他们的指挥了，想躲开都动不了窝儿。到了家的楼下，这时候我们家已经从5栋110一层搬到了12栋303三层。我得支起车后轮让车自己站住，锁了车，双手提着横过来的煤气罐上三楼。普通百姓不知道这个液化石油气和煤气的区别，就跟风叫它煤气罐。实际上，煤气罐更危险，漏了能毒死人，着了火会爆炸，而液化石油气漏点儿没事，着了火也是少量气化部分着火，液化部分受热气化，不会跟着一起着火而发生爆炸。这么轻浮草率地说话，你是谁，你算老几呀？我告诉你们为什么我可以这样"不负责任"地"乱说话"：我的父母亲，姨和姨父都是一辈子搞化学，化工的。我后来也入行化工了，有一段时间，23-29岁的我是煤化工工程师，37岁起当石油化工工程师，现在59岁了。

男孩在那个时代要样样都干。你有几样不干或者没干过，就是劳动表现不好，每年评比三好学生，五好战士什么的，加不上分，不够格，评不上，就会进一步影响到你入不了少先队，那时候叫红小兵，入不了红卫兵，入不了共青团，这就叫落伍了，不先进了。我再说个事儿，作为结束语。因为我家有阳台，几百斤冬储大白菜和白薯等就屯在阳台上，上面盖个破棉被。这样一来我就不用挖菜窖了。而没有挖过菜窖的我，就被人家劳动积极分子盯上了，汇报了，上面就给我一次机会，补上这一课。怎么补呢？我跟另一个类似情况的同学，正好也姓程，程心平，俩人乘坐解放牌大卡车去沙河挖砂子。河床里有筛子，我们俩用铁锹一铲一铲地筛沙子，再高高扬起，把细沙子扔进卡车的后货厢，坐在高高堆起的4吨沙土上，回到本校，再把沙子卸载到沙坑里。那一天，筛4吨，装4吨，卸4吨沙子，是一两个14岁的孩子干的了的活吗？坐在满载卡车货厢的顶上，那上面即没有扶手，也没有安全带，一路颠簸，是一两个孩子所能承受的危险吗？我们俩都默默地认了。那一次劳动，估计补偿了好几年挖菜窖的劳动量了，从此无忧，我们也没有再次被派去干这种或者类似的活儿。到了1983年，大学的全班同学都被迫去北京远郊的荒山上植树并且住在那里，这是一种变相的体罚，用体力劳动和艰苦生活条件洗刷我们逐渐自由化的思想。我没有去。我的毕业论文指导老师谭赞麟先生把他的脚弄断了。他是魏寿昆先生的第一个博士级弟子，舍家一人在钢院就读博士学位，住四层楼上的学生宿舍。我是谭先生的唯一弟子，我必须帮他，背着他，架着他上下楼。为此我逃过了植树劳动，却被同班同学，党员安胜利书记塞了一条大学表现"不爱劳动"的评语，进了我的档案袋。又到了2014年我才又一次到了离沙河不远的地方，计量科学院的墙外挖土。这一次是将我父亲的骨灰盒埋入土中，与我的早早过世的母亲合葬一处，一起往生去了。

9
插队或者上学

　　1967年底1968年初，随着伟大领袖利用大中小学的学生跟他的政敌斗争取得完胜之后，他老人家来了一句，"要复课闹革命"。我正好是7岁上学，赶上了钢院附小招生，就在那里读起了小学。星期一到六，每天早8:00到校，谁也不敢迟到，那是向毛主席早请示的时间。全班起立，班长带头，喊号子："首先，让我们敬祝伟大的导师，伟大的领袖，伟大的统帅，伟大的舵手毛主席万寿无疆"，我们大家跟着挥动手里的毛主席语录，四次挥动，两次呼喊："万寿无疆！万寿无疆！！"班长再带头，喊号子："敬祝伟大领袖毛主席的最亲密的战友林副统帅身体永远健康！"，我们大家跟着挥动手里的毛主席语录，四次挥动，两次呼喊："永远健康！永远健康！！"。然后我们才能坐下来，打开毛主席语录，翻到某页某页，第几段第几行，朗诵毛主席语录。实际上是背诵毛主席语录。因为我们才读小学一年级，连毛主席语录上的字还认不全呢。小学不上不行，中学不上可以，但是要去插队。因为毛主席他老人家还多了一句嘴，"知识青年到农村去，接受贫下中农的再教育，很有必要。"这个表面上的号召实际上是一个诡计，把原来上学的，跟他，帮他闹革命打倒党委及公检法系统的学生们扒拉一堆，打包送到农村去散开了，务农去了，再也集结不了了。这个叫做插队落户，城镇青年的人事，户口插编到农村地方，到农业生产队的编制里面。我的全部表哥表姐都中了这招儿，从北京去山西，陕西，贵州，云南等地插队去了，哪儿穷去哪儿，去稍微好一点的地方显得不够革命，不能吃苦。因为他们是知识分子，继续留在北京以及全国的城镇，对毛是个巨大的威胁。毛在北京已经没有对手了，那么潜在的对手将从学生们，尤其是学生领袖们当中产生。这是政客，玩弄权术的都懂得的"过河拆桥"，"卸磨杀驴"之计，可惜"桥"和"驴"们都不懂。他们纷纷交出权力，给工宣队，军宣队，然后欢天喜地地响应毛主席的号召，到"广阔天地，大有作为"去了。我所上的小学，几乎不存在比我大2岁以上的高班学生。因为1966年开始就没有春季招生了，直到1968年的春季的复课闹革命。原来的小学在校生都到了上初中的年龄。他们升到北京市第93中学去读中学了，93中的原在校生升到了钢院附中去读高中了。三所学校装不下的人，也不论毕业不毕业，以及从93中初中毕业，从钢院附中高中毕业的人，都打起行李下乡插队落户去了。这种毕业生去向，去农村插队，直到1979年才不了了之。1979年初，不打算升学的先去，到9月份没有升上学的，没有考上大学，大专，中专的，都逃不掉去农村插队的命。我们被逼得紧的时候，中学班主任老师拿了一张表，让我们自己填写，其中特别要写明，自己发誓自愿去农村插队落户。校方将此表封存入个人档案。1978年以后，校方不再逼迫自己的毕业生去插队了，临时工悄然兴起。父母所在单位招临时工，每天工资1.50元，正式招工时首先转正他们。我上了四年大学，他们临时工作了四年，其中一个石欣姑娘还帮我做了大学毕业论文的实验室炉前工作，样品制备和论文抄写工作。40年过去了，我们几十位读大学的到处流浪，换工作，出国，到外地的什么样的都有，留钢院本校工作的区区几个；没读大学的我的中学同学们却在钢院工作了一辈子，好几十个，女的55，男的60，都退休了。他们在钢院这所大学里从事的当然不是教学研究工作，而是维持大学校园，这个相当于小城镇建制的生活起居的所有工作，实验室，幼教，财务，基建，电工，水暖工，司机，保安，伙食，后勤，绿化，印刷，教务，房管，甚至保洁等等。这些西方大学校方外包的工作，或者根本不属于大学校方该管的事，中国的大学全管。难怪清华大学的一位校长就曾经狂妄地宣称，他不仅是清华大学的校长，还是清华市的市长。清华，钢院都算是大单位，人口成千上万。中国的大单位等于一个微型城市，这个不是夸张的说法。给国外研究中国问题的专家学者们一个深入研究的路径。对了，在1949年中共建政之前，这种地方还曾经被称做"根据地"，跟土匪占山为王的山寨并无二致。

上学，各位都不能躲开的一件事儿，就是校园霸凌。校园凌霸是全世界的难题，中国的校园里不但有，而且更甚。中国校园霸凌层出不穷的源头是谁呢？笔者认为是家长。家长中的原来是权重位高出身好的，现在加上个钱多的，都变相地鼓励，纵容了他们的孩子在校实施霸凌。文革中，出身好这个因素特别凸显，所谓出身好的就是工农子弟和干部子弟，再加上军人子弟。那么出身不好的，就是我们教师子弟，以及被打倒的干部的子弟了。出身好的欺负，霸凌出身不好的，这成了不成文的规矩。因为我们不敢啊。出身不好，后台不硬，还去欺负人家，在自古至今诛连盛行的中国社会都没有好下场，轻者打了人家，要赔礼道歉写检查领个处分外加出钱给人家疗伤买营养品。我失手用石头打了小学同班同学张士红老弟的眼睛，张家我家都是老师，赔个医药费，全校大会上左副校长把我连批带骂了整整一下午，也就过去了。这是从轻发落。钢院的

体育教师王玉璞的公子王月把工人石师傅的儿子打了
一拳，一拳封眼。这可不得了了。因为王叔叔是国民党
党员，他的儿子王月的出身就差得不能再差了，他爸那
是共产党的死敌呀。王家赔得倾家荡产，王叔叔的罪
名加重到永世不得翻身。这是重的，就是"国民党反动
派地富反坏右派分子的狗崽子向无产阶级红色后代猖
狂报复"，这项大帽子一祭起，你的倒霉家长就会更加
倒霉。作恶多端的霸凌者们不光打人欺负一时弱小的
同学，还肆意破坏他们的书本，文具，自行车等，并且
大肆打砸抢公共财产，辱骂男老师，调戏女老师，殴打
校长，结伙去别的学校打群架。清华大学发生学生用
裤腰带抽打"有阶级立场问题"的教师事件。他们把
该教师绑架到一间封好窗户的，电灯照明的屋子里捆
好让他动也动不了了，这时进来一个自认为出身和阶
级立场都硬邦邦地好的红卫兵小将大学生，手里抡起
裤腰带，第一下就抽坏了屋子里唯一的一盏电灯。室内
进入黑暗，下面几下几十下裤腰带，又叫板儿带，是帆布
硬化制作而成，抡起落下，都伴随着挨打的被绑架者
的惨叫，声震全楼道，甚至传到了室外。施暴者故意不
顾头脸屁股地乱打，使受难者全身重伤害，头脸部伤
情更甚，因为打人者用皮带的金属扣做鞭稍，那个有棱
有角方形的金属扣碰到皮肉头骨牙齿眼睛那里使受刑
者的惨叫声更加凄厉恐怖，那已经不是正常人的抗议

之声了，而是绝望求死的哀鸣，如假包换的鬼哭狼嚎，这样可以让同样被捆绑而来，关在隔壁房间里轮候挨鞭子板儿带的各种"分子"们大惊失色，不寒而栗。钢院发生多起学生及青年教师，原来也曾经是我父亲及其他中年教师的学生们刑讯拷打我父亲以及其他"有问题，拒不交代"的教师和干部的事件。在这里我再次提到我父亲被他们揪住头发往上下双层床的铁架子上反复撞头的"刑"。这次受刑使我父亲大脑受损，记忆力大减，逻辑能力几乎丧失。一个上过清华北大两所全国顶尖大学的人，曾经那么得意地炫耀他的脑子好的人，现在完了，脑子被打坏了。同时受难的几十人及知道这件事的更多的人，甚至是施暴的人一个一个地走了，往生去了。他们的来生还挨打吗？还打人吗？位置互换吗？他们沉默。我不。在我的高中时期，我就把它写进了我的作文，命题作文的题目就是"我的爸爸"。我的笔下，爸爸从非法羁押刑讯他的牢房里刚出来，回家就流着泪对我说，"你不要当老师"。钢院附中最好的语文老师黄河先生给我一个最高分，是优。他也是文革受难者，他被他教过的高中学生打断了腿，因为他是巴山蜀水出来的才子，在抗战时期在国民党的中华民国的临时首都重庆工作，给亲国民党的报纸撰文，编辑。黄河老师还把我的那篇习作交给我父亲读了。据我母亲说，我父亲读后痛哭一场，怎么劝都停不住。在我的记忆力和逻辑推理能力还健在的今天,我要求我自己尽可能详实准确地写出来,而且要印发出来。我这样做,是要当世及后世永不模仿这些前人的过错和罪行。学习历史,就是不要复制历史,不要重演历史。

挨打之后,我父亲失去了尊严,也就失去了活下去的勇气。他不知怎么溜出了关他的房间,溜出了钢院,来到五道口铁轨附近,在那里走来走去,等候过往的火车来,他这是准备卧轨自杀呀。等到天黑,不见火车来,前面又有一个人走来走去,似乎也在等过往的火车,寻求卧轨自杀。这不是柯俊吗?柯俊先生是周恩来总理从英国请回国的金相学大家,金属材料科技的泰斗级专家,中科院院士,在钢院工作,我父亲给他当科学秘书。柯先生有两个学问做得独步天下,也就是世界第一:一个是冶金史,另一个是金相学。不要问他怎么也来自杀了,大家的境遇都差不多,活着失去了尊严还不如死了算了,柯先生还有点深深的自责,怎么抱负科学救国的初心就被共产党给骗了。两人相遇,沉默良久,一起作出了他们要继续人生,哪怕是生不如狗的人生也要活着的重大决定,一错可以,不可再错。于是两人返回钢院,只当什么也没有发生过一样,幸亏什么也没有发生。他们继续接受刑讯审问,交代的东西全部胡编乱造,时间地点人物都对不上头。本来就没有那么回事嘛。校园霸凌事件以学生羁押刑讯斥骂他们的老师,包括世界级大师柯俊和仅在钢院才小有名气的我父亲,作为极端严重的例子,到这里就说完了。其实还没完呢。从校园凌霸中苟活下来的回报是巨大的。特别是当你意外救起不约而同和你一起寻死自杀的顶头上司,并且说服他,也包括你自己不再自杀的那么一回。1978年,柯老在钢院重新掌握了一些权力,他首先派我父亲去西德,看看西方的大学。我爸获得脱产一年学德语,赴德考察2年的美差。其中这个一年学德语彻底治好了他在文革中被拷打致伤的大脑。我父亲当时都47岁了,他17岁时立志留学,考清华没考上,1947上了北大,第二年再考,考上了清华,出国赴美留学在际,1948共产党来了,留学只能被派去苏联,不许自己考试去美国等西方国家了,对我父亲来说,就是哪儿也别去了,读完清华吧。未几,连这个小愿望都破碎了:他就读的清华化学系被院系调整到北大化学系,于是他又回了北大。50年代初期,我父亲读完大学五年,被分配到中科院长春所工作。由于他在大学学习的时候过分活跃,在清华任学生会人事部长(当时的学生会主席叫朱镕基,后来当过20年右派,再后来当过十年总理);在北大当学生会的文艺部长。就被北大校方任命为小组长,带着北京分配到长春去的另外四名大学毕业生向长春所所长报到。所长首先进行了政审,5个人里面有四名是共产党员,就是带队的我父亲不是党员。这可是反了,党是领导,怎么会被领导呢？于是所长把我父亲打回北大，留下了那四位党员大学毕业生。北大给我父亲来了个二次分配，他才进了北京钢院。钢院才建院，什么样儿的人都要。他就在这里工作了一辈子。那四位留在长春工作的人是怎么埋怨我父亲的，从生活条件来说，是北京越来越好，中央集权制的中央所在地嘛。长春却越来越差，最差的时候长春军区司令兼政委陈锡联，副手毛泽东的侄子毛远新在东北三省上马管军，下马管民的1975年，配给市民每个月三两油，出了东北，全国各地的城镇居民都是每个月5两油。陈司令因此得了个"陈三两"的外号。1983年，我的东北同学刘长武给我讲他们在家乡的苦日子：油不够，炒菜时就后加油。用一根筷子先蘸水，再去油瓶子里蘸油，然后往"炒"熟的菜里面一搅和，这个菜就算是炒的，而不是熬的啦，还美其名曰"后老婆油"。油瓶子里的油位不降反升，是因为油下面的水积在瓶子里顶高了油位！北京长春两地差别越大，他们的埋怨就越深，就差说我爸坑他们了。后来"坑人"的报应来到了我头上。1986年我读硕士毕业了，虽然分配留校在北京，但是要从留校的我们十几位同学里坑一个人去东北中苏边境，任中央机关讲师团的讲师一年。我，就是那个挨坑的，有一点角色变化是，这次挖坑的是党员毕业生顾伯良书记，而往坑里跳的我不是党员。回来说我父亲和柯俊。现在文革结束了，柯老要求钢院给我父亲升教授, 脱产学一年学德语, 去德国考察大学1-2年, 顺便替他行使权利, 在钢院和德国亚琛工业大学结成姊妹学校的校际合作协议上签字背书。这个学一年德语居然治愈了我父亲在文革时挨打的头部外伤导致记忆力衰弱的顽疾。一年后, 1979年, 我父亲作为钢院公派暨柯俊私人代表赴德国成行, 我也顺利考入钢院我父亲的专业, 家里双喜临门, 我父亲临行前还再三嘱咐我和家人, 这一段时间谁也不许惹任何麻烦。而我都想好了要去学校霸凌一下, 试试身手了呢。幸亏父亲刹了一下我的车。又过了两年, 学校的广播里传来"喜讯", 在全体师生信仰危机的关头, 柯老长期申请加入中国共产党的愿望实现啦! 这是在他65岁, 大权旁落后才实现的, 我们几个在读大学生都觉得这是对科学大神的一种亵渎。同年, 柯老的科学秘书, 我的父亲第一次考察德国完毕, 回到钢院, 向前来诱他入党的系党委书记, 他曾经的学生段淑珍女士说, 他要撤回他的入党申请书, 因为德国一程已经使他脱胎换骨, 改变了信仰。未几, 钢院冶金系的林宗采先生介绍我父亲加入中国民主同盟。林宗采家兄或者大舅子是京汉铁路二七大罢工时牺牲的烈士林相谦, 因为林先生的太太, 人称林大姐, 恰好也姓林, 林相谦是他们俩谁的哥哥, 我搞不清楚。没关系, 他们的儿子大头哥比我大好几岁, 文革耽误了他的功课, 就找我来补习一下, 我还因此当上了义务补习老师，在12栋302，我家隔壁的中学同班女同学刘小江家给他们俩上过补习课呢。在民盟，我父亲效力于费孝通主席，一直作到民盟北京市主委，民盟中央委员呢。在任期内，他要跟班中共统战部长严明复。严是八个民主党派的太上皇，各党派的主席，如费孝通，史良等都必须听命于他。这与西方党派，执政党反对党什么的根本就不一样，它不平等。这是另一种意义上的霸凌，政治霸凌。这种霸凌的具体表现是，中共统战部长强迫各个民主党派在他们自己的党章里的第一条明确写好，该党或者盟，或者社，本党，本盟，本社拥护共产党，接受共产党的领导。而其他自己想成立的组织，则根本成立不起来，因为共产党就不允许，不批准他们成立，结果现存的八个所谓的民主党派无一例外，全部都是1949年及之前成立的，苟延残喘到今天的，外国称之为花瓶党的组织。各党派的头头都是明显的老资格，不愿意臣服于共产党的什么统战部长，结果就是我父亲这样的秘书级，副官级人员在同共产党的部长大人斡旋。钢院里面也有民主党派，也就有共产党方面的统战部长。这些从中央到地方，大大小小的统战部长们，就是货真价实的霸凌实施者，他们一直霸凌到了你们的信仰和政治倾向里面，并且以此为乐，以此为业，以此为职，还领工资，奖金，分房子什么的都有，并且以此为晋身之阶。研究中国问题的专家们，请从统战部长处着手，这是我给你们另辟的蹊径。共产党是怎么占领学校，占领医院，占领研究院，设计院，检查院，法院，等部门，并且实行有效统治的。都会在这里找到答案。

10

街头暴力之一，骂大街

　　下面讲一些文革中的街头暴力，骂大街，游街，烧汽车和查架。

　　骂大街一般由比较泼辣的妇女参加，其他人只是围观，并且在精彩处送上一场哄笑。泼辣妇女的泼辣之处，恰好在观众。观众多时更泼辣的妇女胜出，平时貌似柔弱的妇女，往门口外一站，腰一叉，嘴一张，能演出一场长达几个小时的独角独白戏，语言变化多端，用语不带重样儿的，是高级骂。挨骂的如果不应战，往往示弱，不跟她一般见识了，吃的是哑巴亏。可是挨骂的如果也是这么泼辣，比如说，对方骂到她了，骂到她的短处了，骂到她的亲人了，而她实在是忍不住了，就跳出来站在对方面前破口大骂。独角戏变成了多角戏，更多的揭短，更难听的骂人话，疾速对骂，巧妙接下茬儿都很精彩，有的堪称绝伦。

　　"我是不是比你强？"

"你就是墙! 你除了篱笆全是墙! "

巧妙地运用了同音异义字, 强和墙, 把对方从人人惧怕的强大的强, 一下子变成了人人讨厌的砖头的墙。高级骂。其人弗能应也。

"你滚蛋! "

"滚就滚。滚鸡蛋, 滚鸭蛋, 滚出一颗手榴弹, 炸死你个王八蛋! "

这个对骂使两人都变成了蛋, 哺乳动物变成了卵生动物。低级骂。

郭文贵在近年的直播中, 引用了一句骂大街的话, "放你的罗圈儿屁! "不过与民谚有些出入。我的版本是: "放你的萝卜丝儿拐弯儿屁!" 。罗圈儿屁比较费解, 萝卜丝儿拐弯儿屁就比较接近生活。你一个健康的人, 吃一顿萝卜, 再喝口热茶, 保准会不停地放屁, 文雅的说法, 叫做回肠荡气, 还是成语哪, 就是顺着肠子拐弯儿的屁, 弄不好还会产生食物中毒现象, 打嗝放屁都是轻的, 重的要找医生, 去医院呢。

"吃萝卜, 喝热茶, 气得大夫满街爬。"童谣禁止不当食物搭配, 防止食物中毒, 贡献不小。

童谣和民谚加入骂大街的章节, 似乎不妥, 降低了前两者的名分。但是我要爬格子挣那个稿费, 这么写到一起, 有人看。分开写, 看倒是也有人看, 就是少。

"我向伟大领袖毛主席保证,林副统帅出事了。这件事是真的。"我们几个孩子躲在已经落成的,林彪号令我们在自己家附近修的防空洞里,听一个比我们大几岁的男孩刘涛说。

不久,美国的国务卿基辛格博士访华,并且带来了一些美国记者。全国人民为了招架这几位敌人,美国人,作了充分的应答准备,官方要求是不卑不亢。

美国人如果跟你打招呼,叫你"哈喽!",你应该回答"哈你个萝卜!你搂我也搂!"当然,这是民间版。

美国人似乎听说了林彪出了事,就到处打听。问到一个北京口音,尤其是儿话音浓重的人,你们的林副统帅怎么了?得到的回答是"隔儿屁了。"这个词儿不在新华字典里,也不在康熙字典里,可是难倒了美国人,而全北京,乃至全中国人都知道,"隔儿屁着凉大海棠"就是死了的意思,而且是对死者死亡事件不恭的表述。当然,这也是民间版。我的著作,我的大作鲜有官方的官样文章,目的是让同是草根的大众了解一下,登堂入室的普通话,白话文都是另有市场的,这个广大的市场存在于民间,而民间的使用,才是一种语言的生命力之所在。

骂大街的层次有些讲究,直接骂"你妈B"的就是严重了,或者是言重了。钢院5栋有个孩子叫王根,其父在清河钢铁厂工作,没什么钱还爱喝酒。他经常让儿子去打散装白酒，0.13元一两，钱多了，酒瘾上来了，就让儿子打二两酒。"根儿啰，二两！"是他爸爸的指令。王根好脾气，谁都这么喊他，他却从来不生气。很快，他爸爸的金句又唱响钢院，随后唱响全国，并且流传至今。当年的父子对话是：

"爸！给我买双鞋吧。"

没什么钱的爸爸无语。

"爸！给我买双鞋嘛。"根儿啰央求。

"买你妈腿！"

这个"你妈腿儿"从此就代替了阴毒的"你妈B"。今天的直播里还在骂人时唱起。这是明证。再后来，钢院的5栋搬来一家，从西北来，大概是姓方，这家的小男孩非常可爱，没有受到欺负，还跟着北京孩子学骂人。"你妈B"没学到家，弄出来一个"你妈给"。从此，欢乐的大院子弟们"妈给妈给"的即可以称呼他这个外地小坏蛋，又可以骂其他小伙伴，成了最温和的骂街术语。今天，骂人也不再直接骂娘了，而是以妹妹代替，"管你妹啊！"，"刷你妹！"等，语言也在进化，中国人民问候别人家的老年或者年长妇女的陋习转变成了问候别人的妹妹，也不知道这个被问候的人有没有妹妹。

11

街头暴力之二，游街

　　游街是一件很负面的热闹事，是文革中批斗大会的延伸。封建时期有之，但是没有见过。文革时的游街，我们几乎人人都见过。文革伊始，共和国的刘少奇主席的夫人王光美被清华大学的学生揪斗，就开始了游街的暴力。这个对王光美女士的重伤害的后台是江青。江青是毛的最后一任夫人。王被游街时，项链变成了一串乒乓球，她一个物理学硕士，第一夫人变成了菜刀们当众施虐取乐的对象。一般的老百姓一旦被揪过去游街，丑恶，丑化，丑闻，私密等就全部公开了。游街的过程中，揪着被游街人的所谓正义者以及任何其他能接近他们的人都可以任意击打被游街的人，在他身上做些令人作呕的事情，撒尿，吐痰，抹屎，涂鸦，造谣，谩骂，诅咒，笑话，诋毁，诽谤什么的都有。这些人在犯罪而不自知，或者故意犯罪以表现他们最革命，对反革命毫不手软。也有些小偷流氓被游街，而女流氓或者"作风不正派"的女教师,女干部被游街时,脖子上都挂着一双破鞋。于是"破鞋"成了她们专有的统一的称谓,"搞破鞋"则不限男女。2013年我回国探望年迈的父亲,早上陪他去钢院的大操场"早锻炼",其实是去会一会老同事,老伙伴,老朋友,以互相证明一下他们还都活着而已。90多岁的老干部,当过新四军华南纵队队员的孝步厚老人冲口而出:"那个破鞋又说什么啦?"他骂谁他们一伙老人都知道,当时美国的国务卿希拉里比较烦人,烦中国人。可是我还不知道,就问左右,引来几个老头子的哄堂大笑。身体不用锻炼,大家都开心顺气就是最好的成果。在他们当中,可尽是当年文革期间,在同一个大操场被游过街的,被批斗的人。他们现在互相取乐,当时谁谁谁是个什么窘态,下跪,自黑者有之。我转移话题,更加低俗地给他们加点乐子,叙述了一个当今上海姑娘征婚的标准:叫做三个180. 在场的物理教研室主任,我的热学老师兰之斌先生哆哆嗦嗦地问了个详细,他罹患帕金森症。这第一个180是,我说,男方有180平方米的房子,而且已经供完房贷,不用老娘跟你节衣缩食,吃方便面省下钱来供房子;第二个180是,男方的身高有180公分。这是要求婚后带得出去,体面见人,不能是半残的,就是对身高175公分以下的男人的蔑称,更不能是残废的,就是身高165公分以下的男子;这第三个180嘛,以毫米计量。您是物理老师，对尺度有所了解吧？我卖了个关子，兰老师哈哈大笑，笑得脸都红了，表示他秒懂了。轮到其他人问左右啦。主动游街其乐无穷，被动游街苦不堪言。苦乐参半，颐养天年。

12

街头暴力之三, 烧汽车

文革中烧汽车是在北京的东华门。

从我奶奶爷爷家走出来奶子府胡同, 现在叫康健胡同, 再走出去灯市口大街, 往南走, 就到了一条更大的大街, 叫王府井的地方。王府井还没到, 就是一个十字路口, 叫王府井东华门。这里马路特别宽, 封建王朝的官员们进故宫见皇帝, 要是骑马来的, 就要在此下马, 并且把马交给下属或者马弁, 牵到皇家马厩的客栈去饮水, 休息, 吃草, 松马肚带, 钉马掌, 展示鞍轿, 甚至谈场恋爱, 配个种什么的。人类豢养宠物, 如果分室内室外的话, 马当然是户外第一宠, 猫就是室内第一宠了, 狗两头都有点, 算院宠吧。此话另当别论。我们要说的是汽车和烧汽车。现代的汽车就是古代的马。

在这里烧新时代的汽车, 别有一番"伟大的现实意义", 结合皇家招待奴才官员的客栈马厩所在地, 还有其"深刻的历史意义"。这都是文革术语。小汽车, 那时候还叫小轿车，与封建社会里给达官贵人乘坐的轿子，现在才被取缔了十几年的轿子遥相呼应，是文革前，文革中，文革后又十年的高级官员专用的交通工具，都是权利的象征。烧了它，你们就清楚地接受了一个信号：这回的革命，是针对高干的。我到现在还特别激动地描述烧车过程，给大家介绍一个仔细的"点火烧车工艺流程"，但是希望大家不要模仿。学习历史，不模仿它。

轿车的后行李箱，或者车内后窗前的三角区里，常放置一把鸡毛掸子。普通家用的最多2尺长，可是汽车用鸡毛掸子的手柄短，鸡毛多而且长，至少有三尺。文革的那次烧汽车是把司机和乘车的高干赶下车，当着他们的面点燃汽车的。没人的时候怎么办？打破车窗，把那个鸡毛掸子拿出来，杵到汽油箱里蘸些汽油出来，点燃这个鸡毛掸子，再把它插回到汽车的后座上。那里有"柴禾"，就是座椅的面料和里子，下面还有汽油箱，那是更多的"柴禾"。不一会儿，汽车的内外都燃起大火，冒出黑烟，烧不到半小时，这辆汽车就完全报废啦。你们来看看，这种暴行的成本，最多是2分钱，一盒火柴的钱。可是烧掉，破坏了多少钱，造成多少空气污染，废车拉走，占地堆放又是多少？以十万计。最不可饶恕的是，烧车人无罪溜跑了。革命赋予他这个烧车权力吗？正是。文革开始时，有一伙红卫兵来了一次冲中南海，去抓捕在那里工作的周恩来总理的事件。这个也是街头暴力。可惜被中南海的持枪警卫挡住了。那次冲中南海的，有一个何世民先生，后来成了我所在的办公室的主任，我的顶头上司。他的"光辉事迹"被人装进了他的档案袋，为此他不能出国。每次政审都因为这个而不合格，不合格就别出国。他的出国名额就被人拿去自己出国用掉了。谁呢？就是本单位的党支部书记李中和。等到1989年1月轮到我该出国了，李中和书记就故伎重演，把政审不给合格的威胁压到了我的头上，从1月拖延政审期到了5月。1989年5月的北京，政治气候多么不确定啊！你不给我政审，有人及时出现了，就像天使一般帮我。从外地内蒙古包头钢铁公司大型国企来北京冶金部做官升任司长的某人带进北京一位官太太。官太太原来在包头也是官，叫汪仲谏处长，来北京继续做官，就安插进了我们煤炭部。部里编制已经满额，装不下她，就把她"下放"到我所在的煤炭工业环境监测总站当处级常务站长，官阶正好比那个正科级李书记李副站长高整整一级。她本人亲自深入我的办公室化学实验室计算机房兼新婚居住集合体的小房间，当天当面对我完成了结论是合格的政审，使我将将能够逃命，躲过了北京街头的举世震惊的军事血腥镇压学生行动，我于5月31号乘中国首都北京到苏联首都莫斯科的国际列车逃往最终目的地，西德亚琛。要不是这位汪处长及时通过对我的政审保送我出国，我还在中国北京闹事，说不定坐牢的不仅有后面将提到的钢院合作社头目刘瘸子和钢院子弟苏钢，还会有我程迅呢。

　　闪回倒叙。1989年4月，北京的大学生又一次冲中南海，典型的街头暴力，却又一次失败，还挨了打。如果原总书记胡耀邦之死是导火索的话，那么这次冲中南海就应该是点燃导火索，发展成为波澜壮阔的8964运动的火种。1989年的6月，在北京的大街上又烧了一次汽车，不过这次受害的汽车，大部分是军车，　还有几辆公交车。成串儿的军车在和平时期到全国政治中心首都北京的政治中心天安门附近去挨烧，这个逻辑不通啊。钢院合作社的领导人刘瘸子被抓去坐牢了，他往已经点燃的军车火堆里加了一撮垃圾，权作柴禾，遂构成街头暴力犯罪。我奇怪，为什么菜刀们烧汽车就可以逍遥法外，而非菜刀们就得坐牢？　钢院5栋207的苏钢是在钢院外读书的学生，钢院教工子弟。　他也因此8964被抓去坐牢了，他才十几岁呀。这两位是我都认识的，住在同一个院子里的，甚至住在同一个门洞的，以街头暴力反抗街头暴力的人。可以理解为他们在替我坐牢。因为8964之前的几十个夜晚，我可都是在北京街头度过的。大狱里传出来的消息令人少安毋躁，一个老公安出来召集并主持"64犯人的家属，家长会"：凡8964闹事被判决在本监狱服刑者在狱中得到了狱卒和难友们的双重礼遇，就是说，尊他们为假暴徒，真英雄。早晚出去了，不是平反昭雪，就是落实政策。这是我的话。不过事情，在我写作这个章节的时候，2019年5月间，30年都快过去了，平反昭雪和落实政策都还没有影子。8964那次坦克也去了。但是没烧着坦克。这不是因为共军的坦克结实，就是因为放火的人不知道怎样点燃一辆坦克。共军的坦克是烧柴油的哈。鸡毛掸子的没有，汽油的没有，窟窿眼的也没有，坦克里面连可燃物质都没有。鸡毛掸子蘸柴油是烧不着的。其实，8964那次该烧的，就是这些坦克。所以，坦克上战场打仗，赢不赢的没准儿，而坦克上大街镇压平民乃至暴民，去一回赢一回，去两次胜两次。暴力从街头烧汽车开始，以极端暴力军用坦克血腥碾压平民中止。坦克进首都北京，在全国政治中心的最具政治符号的地点，天安门前的长安街以及其他街道上，在充满抗议的人群当中行进，则是最厉害的街头暴力。比这种暴力，暴政更反人类的暴力，笔者见识少，没有见过，只是听说过，布拉格之春，西藏首府拉萨都发生过类似街头暴力事件，就是坦克开进城。但是笔者坚信，能够完美战胜暴力的，不是更加暴力，而是某种或者某几种非暴力力。笔者仅举8964之前和之后两例：1986年菲律宾首都马尼拉街头，荷枪士兵被上帝感召，撕下自己身上佩戴的总统卫队袖标，调转枪口，支持民众，导致独裁者马科斯总统下台流亡。所幸之事是，市民，军人和马科斯总统都信仰同一位上帝, 同一位圣母; 苏联始于1917年阿芙勒尔号巡洋舰炮击冬宫, 终止于1991年前往莫斯科镇压民众的苏联红军坦克驶进莫斯科却未开一枪一炮, 反而被叶利辛踩在脚下, 坦克手的内心被和平演变反共的理念所征服。人类真的进化, 文明了。在此强调一下, 拥有暴力手段的人, 不管他在何时何地, 什么职位, 坚持使用暴力的都是懦夫, 而放弃这个暴力需要更大的勇气。我们现在把目光引向2019年6月9日至9月29日每个周末的香港街头, 那里发生着数十万到两百万市民和平游行, 连美国总统川普都没见过这么好秩序的超大规模游行。而此前夕, 就有人引燃汽油燃烧弹, 拿棍子打人, 把和平行动引向街头暴力, 把香港市民对中共的不满引向他们对中国军警伪装的香港警察的愤怒, 为中共及其军队再次变装, 化装出动实施武装暴力镇压做好借口。好毒好邪恶! 我在这里交代几种结局: 第一就是兵变。港警也好, 伪警也好, 军人也好, 他们手中一旦有了枪, 枪膛里一旦有了子弹, 往哪儿打枪还真不敢说。第二就是镇压。镇压香港成功将导致国际制裁中共, 而按下葫芦浮起瓢, 以后"戡乱"其他地方就会显得苍白无力。到那时候, 才是有中共的地方"天下大乱"了。第三就是软着陆。共军或者共匪和平撤离香港, 签发一个28年不再犯港公告。这个第三种结局都做不到, 或者没人去试试, 咱们大家还真不如我下面要说的, 查架打群架的小流氓呢!

13
街头暴力之四,查架打群架

查架打群架往往以和平收场,很少以暴力终结。把查架算成街头暴力,有点勉强。但是,每次查架的现场发展的不确定性,令人们无比激动,见识场面。查得好的架打不起来,双方握手言和,通常是某一方请来的人在江湖名分较另一方高,或者是同门,而辈分不同。这就打不起来。江湖规矩大,等级森严,盗亦有道指的可能就是这个。我所在的中学班里,发生了唯一的一次查架,就是钢院子弟王进跟地院子弟谷金铸查起架来了。地院在文革中响应毛主席的号召,把北京地质学院搬到湖北去了。留守处的人没守住,地院里又来了航测大队等几个单位,但是人还是少,地院附中办不下去了,各种住地院的子弟,统称地院子弟就散养到周边的附中附小去上学,我们钢院附中就接受了我们这一届的地院子弟。一般地院子弟客座其他学校读书时,都很老实,可是这个谷金铸就不安分。校长和老师都怂恿他出来闹，象个小丑那样闹。为什么他可以胡闹，而别人不可以？原来是他有一个哥哥叫谷金钟，与钢院附中的文革后期的副校长，高干子弟谢国栋一起干过兵团。兵团的事以后讲，高干子弟的事就不讲了，谢国栋逼着我的刚来月经的女同学们下水田弯腰劳动的事上面已经讲过了。他挺浑的哈。看来谷金钟和谢国栋是和的来，谢就惠顾谷的弟弟谷金铸。谢把那么不安分的谷金铸生生打造成后进变先进的典型，令他在全校大会上发言，介绍活学活用毛泽东思想，改邪归正，立志远大，严格要求自己的先进事迹。这就构成了几个钢院子弟的嫉妒羡慕恨。首先是罗建国。他在全班到钢院大操场出早操时因为迟到被谷金铸耻笑了，罗冲上去就给谷一个耳光。事后罗交了检讨，而他的检讨的底稿是另一个钢院子弟，也就是我打的。我的文字功力从那时候已经开始展露，只是还不知道用该到正道上，还是歪路上，叫做不明是非，算是缺点吧。然后是又一个钢院子弟王进跟谷金铸查架。王和谷没有动手，两个人忽然就都不来上学了，各自在自己的群里群外找打手。不过那个时候没有群，叫圈子也不对。圈子是当时对不太检点的青年女子的蔑称。叫什么呢？不知道。双方到了约定的日子，到了约定的场所，就是钢院附小西侧和9栋之间的小树林里。那里是约定俗成的战场，现在是老干部活动站。笔者也在那里失手误伤了同班的张士红同学。本来没有打架，而是双方自动分成两排，在下学的路上互掷石块儿，美其名曰做游戏，结果先打中了参战的黄春雷的身体，又击中了没有参战的路人张士红的眼睛。这已经是第二次提到他了。那就再次深表歉意。也是在同一个战场上，还发生了既是叔侄，又是同班同学，还住同一个16斋的钢院厨师子弟王永刚王国正打斗事件。那次见识到了几招中国武术，因为王永刚会这几招，就把什么都不会的他叔给打败了。在此的打架还有那么几次，师老师骂哭陈继跃同学，这在文革期间很罕见，一般都是学生骂老师，打校长，调戏女教师等。这里发生过王永刚脚踩头着地的李选的头，踢他的脑袋。李选可能被踢醒了。后来的他一路专家博导地当上了北大教授，专门治疗人类大脑的内患外伤。他可以算是校园凌霸受害者当中最因祸得福的一个了。其他人有多少身心俱毁？钢院采矿系教授杨泽器的独子杨同被一伙人群殴至开了瓢儿，就是脑袋被打破了一个洞，血窜得老高。非钢院子弟魏彦林被同一伙人群殴，也被他们开了瓢儿，也是血窜得老高。他们的颅损伤加上缝针治疗导致他们失智。这伙人当中的杨勇打到了我的头上，让我鼻血窜出才罢休，最后失智的倒是他杨勇。1979年我上大学，惊见杨勇在给大学教室扫地打开水做杂役临时工呢。这些都是发生在这个小树林里。还是在这同一个战场，校方组织战争演习，上课上到一半，警报响起，全校师生要尽快躲出建筑物,到空地上集结,而集结地就是这个战场。那是一次失败的军事演习。800名师生拥堵在钢院附小的二层楼道里,大家争抢两头的楼梯,夺路而逃,不幸的曾星小朋友被踩到了众人的脚下。也不知道多少人踩了他多少脚,他的头上脸上身上都被踩花了,眼球从眼眶里挤了出来,恐怖至极。

回来继续叙述王谷查架。王请来了打手,江湖浪名娃子,谷请来了另一位打手,名高望重,披一条长长的白色围巾,戴了墨镜,留了长发。他用我们当时都还没有具备的男低音说,还打吗?娃子无语。不到1分钟,未经动手过招儿,事件结束,胜者抚摸着娃子的肩膀退场了。场外的交易,事前订约,事后履约什么的,不尽其祥。胜者谷金铸却再也没有回来上学,败者王进回校后,参加了高考准备班。钢院附中永远是我们钢院子弟的。他从初一到高三始终坐在前两排,是老师照顾得非常好的学生。高考发榜,王进同学以全班第一名,340分的成绩考取南开大学物理系,还是我们班最好的。

14
过年

　　过年对孩子们来说是大喜事。放鞭炮，好玩不贵，0.21元/百头小鞭，就是最小号的鞭炮。用火捻编起来，用竹竿或木棍挑起来，燃放下端的火捻，百响清脆的爆炸声，声声入耳，腾起一团烟雾。这是一种有钱人家的玩法。我们在整个春节期间，也许只有区区一两元的炮仗钱，哪里肯一点百响图个一时痛快，而后全年干瞪眼，看别人家的孩子放鞭炮？放二踢脚，放双响炮，放麻雷子，放烟花，钻天猴什么的？我们都是把百响小鞭小心翼翼地拆解成一放一响的单发炮仗，然后取一段一二尺长的棉线，那时候叫小线，纳鞋底子用的，现在根本没地方买去。引燃棉线，其功能象香一样，保持阴火不灭。点每一头鞭炮都用这个棉线火捻向鞭炮导火索一怼，然后跑开，堵上耳朵，等它啪的一声爆炸。胆子大的孩子，如我自己，从来是左手持火棉绳，右手的食指和拇指尖捏住炮仗的两端，什么道理？烧得太快的导火索会马上引爆鞭炮，来不及扔出去的鞭炮在手里爆炸，会炸到手，震到耳朵，你就变成了大家取笑的对象了。而捏住炮仗的两端，可以堵住导火索一路燃烧进入炮仗体内，熄灭它，让炮仗只能脱手后爆炸。这是一种自我保安措施或者安全拿法。脱手扔出去，这个堵就取消了，导火索的燃烧的路自动通了，鞭炮该炸就炸，到它该去的地方去爆炸，对自己安全，大家都取乐。

15
有钢种锅的修理

　　修理行业是一个无所不包的地方。可以说，有人有东西的地方就有修理业。我小的时候没有见过口腔矫形，脊椎矫形，外形整容等。除此之外，差不多都有所目睹。

　　修钢笔的。有一则侯宝林的相声调侃他们修钢笔的。说看见对面来了个人，上衣口袋里只插着一枝笔的，那是识字的学生；插着两枝笔的，那是教书先生；而别着三枝笔的，甭问，那准是修笔的。钢笔，以其笔尖所用的材料得名，有钢片上加铱的叫铱金钢笔，而加金的就直接叫金笔。笔尖的材料决定了这枝笔的价值。英制派克牌钢笔最有名。是最高档的钢笔。2003年我去英国牛津大学，顺访在那里的文具店，发现早已淘汰了的派克牌钢笔还有卖的呢，150英镑一枝。那叫一个神气。我不敢买。不是因为兜儿里没有钱，而是怕它坏了没地方修去。修笔的行业近20年来从人们的视

310

野中消失了。与它结伴而行的是修钟表的店铺。进门一看，一般只有一位师傅，即管修表又管客户服务，全面负责接活儿，送活儿，收钱找零钱，复写单据。他的眼睛上夹着一个放大镜之类的东西，很有行业标志的样子。桌子上，精巧的修表工具，镊子，改锥，钳子，小台钳以及一小铁盒煤油。那里的煤油是洗表芯用的。机械钟表（当时根本没有电子钟表）用久了以后，就要拿到钟表行附设的修表摊位，或者独立的修表铺去拆洗一下，去掉油泥，加上高级润滑油，盖上钟表背面的盖子，完活儿。好家伙，5块一个哪！修表师傅顺便调一下表芯里的发条弹簧限制阀，使其走时准确起来。怎么判断你的钟表准不准呢？这是广播电台的事儿。每小时电台都播放一组定时，正时音，"嘟-嘟-嘟-嘟-嘟-嘀-"，然后是男或者女播音员的报时："刚才最后一响，是北京时间X点正。"　下一个是眼镜店。戴眼镜要修的是人的视力。很多人有先天性近视眼或者远视眼。这是一种眼疾，得治。但是在文革期间那么多人就忍着，就不去配戴眼镜矫正一下。为什么呢？那时候的人有一种观念，戴眼镜的学问大。而学问大在当时就是一种罪恶。"1，2，3，4，5，6，7，戴眼镜的没出息"童谣如是说。"小四眼"是一个蔑称性的外号。我们班只有一个徐力同学获此"殊荣"，没想到他戴着眼镜考上了军校，毕业后戴着眼镜当了军官，负责指挥灯丝式电子管驱动的苏式萨姆6地对空导弹, 保卫伟大祖国的首都北京的领空, 是现在称做"逆袭"的典范。几十年过去了, 同学们在聚会时, 居然有个卢跃同学叫不上他徐力的名字, 而是直呼其外号"小四眼"相认。这种有眼病不治的状况到了1975年有所改善, 邓小平替代重病的周恩来总理出来主持中央政府的工作, 他要从抓教育入手, 撤换了教育部的革委会主任, 使教育部长周荣鑫复职, 他还没有来得及撤换清华北大革委会头头, 老毛的迟群同志, 及爱姬谢静宜, 就又下去了。我可倒了他的霉。因为我在那个期间配戴了一副近视眼镜。刚开始有点示威性质地在全班同学面前戴上了眼镜, 改头换面, 励精图治, 好好学习, 带个头哈。结果老邓下去了, 政治风向变了, 把我晒那儿了。我在班委团支部联席会议上被内定为"走白专道路的典型", 欲置于班会批判对象, 择日点名, 斗倒斗臭。这是背着我整我的一次严重事件。因为我即不是班干部, 也不是团干部, 无权参加这个联席会议。这次整我的班会没开成。1976年是政治瞎忙年, 周恩来1月, 朱德5月, 毛泽东9月去世, 唐山7月大地震, 华国锋10月"宫廷政变"等大人物大事件一个接一个地发生, 谁顾得过来整我这个小布喇子呀? 我只是任第四小组的组长及谁都不愿意上的崇洋媚外课程, 英语课科代表。第四小组被我私下里称做"四野", 遥遥对应中国人民解放军主力, 林彪的第四野战军。四野击败了国民革命军正规军数百万，把他们从中国大陆赶到台湾去了。我还自比林彪呢。在班里，我的四野是一群名声不好，表现不好，不受待见的男孩子们。我们全班下乡劳动，1, 3, 5三个组的女生吃不了的定量都往2组6组另外两个男生组送。我的"四野"没有女生的青睐，饭不够吃就去打野食。打饭的时间到了，我坐镇指挥，几人向左去随大流打伙房做的饭菜馒头窝头粥，另几个人晚走几步向右，去果园庄稼地里摘些偷些半生不熟的果实来充饥。出了事由我向带队老师王雪交代，检讨。这个主意不怎么样。吃了青涩的果子我们感到更饿了。我的四野出了个打遍钢院无敌手的罗建国，他爸爸是保卫科，武装部的头头，是可以带枪上班的那种人。罗建国在全班全年级去北京边戌学军时假装嗓子痛，企图跟担任班级医药卫生员的王树玲女同学要几片润喉口含药片，甜味甘美，与薄荷的清凉俱存，无糖果时期这个也好吃哈。结果被聪慧的王树玲识破其看病是假，打坏主意跟女生交往是真---他这个嗓子怎么不红不肿呀？她就杏眼圆睁，给罗来了一针注射，估计这是她此生唯一的一次行医。其实针剂里面就是蒸馏水，啥药也没有。王树玲就是想让罗建国挨上一针，疼一下，以后别来找麻烦。疗效还真不错。从此罗建国不打本班女生的坏主意了，而是转向比我们小一岁，却跟我们同年级的"戴帽班"的女生去了。

我的四野又出了个北京市地铁总设计师程心平。他一考二考三考，坚决要上大学，契而不舍的"大西"终于考进了北方交大后，他爸爸仅仅奖励了他一瓶汽水，抠门抠得有些喜感。我的四野还出了个全班的男生首富郭广明。我的四野也出过北京市乒乓球无冕之王王小东，以及他的陪练之一，也就是我。我跟他的另一位陪练一起修理他，直到他可以挑战并战胜冠军们。这个陪练叫周建。他现在可好了，位居北京昆泰集团老总，正的。

这个对人身体的修理就是行医；对人脑筋的修理就是教育和考试；对人的体育动作，体育比赛技战术的修理就是教练。它们都是广义的修理行业。

说到本篇章的题目，里面提到了一个名字，叫钢种锅。它就是铸铝锅。金属铝进入千家万户是文革前不久的事。先见到美军的铝皮军用水壶，它是军用的。用收破烂收来的废旧金属本来就少，废旧铝就更加罕见。慢慢的，就有了国产版的铸铝军民两用水壶。其外形跟美军版的一样，跟英军版的就很不一样。再后来，1980年以后才知道，人家美军的后勤厉害，喝水可以喝可口可乐，行军打仗也可以不用自备水壶。到了20年以前才知道，共军的后勤也厉害，喝水可以喝贵州茅台，演习也可以不用自备水壶。行军，打仗？没有这回事。当然，这是笑话。

军队坏了修理军队，党坏了修理党。菜刀们的刃值得我们去锵吗？

全文完。

2019-09-29

多伦多

CPSIA information can be obtained
at www.ICGtesting.com
Printed in the USA
LVHW051101271219
641843LV00014B/205/P

9 780228 818953